CHECK

YOUR ENGLISH

A FOUR-SKILLS
GRAMMAR PRACTICE BOOK

Richard MacAndrew
Jon Blundell

Student's Book 1

MACMILLAN
PUBLISHERS

© Text Richard MacAndrew and Jon Blundell 1990
© Illustrations Macmillan Publishers Ltd 1990

All rights reserved. No reproduction, copy or transmission
of this publication may be made without written permission.
No paragraph of this publication may be reproduced, copied
or transmitted save with written permission or in accordance
with the provisions of the Copyright Act 1956 (as amended).
Any person who does any unauthorised act in relation to
this publication may be liable to criminal prosecution and
civil claims for damages.

First published 1990

Published by *Macmillan Publishers Ltd*
London and Basingstoke
and associated companies

ISBN 0–333–49228-5

Printed in Hong Kong

Design: Jim Weaver Design
Illustrations: Jordan and Jordan

A CIP catalogue record for this book is available from
the British Library.

ACKNOWLEDGEMENTS
**The Authors and Publishers wish to thank the following
sources for permission to reproduce copyright material:**
Controller of HMSO; Geographers' A-Z Map Co. Ltd;
News of the World.
Photographs by courtesy of:
Barnaby's Picture Library; Camera Press Ltd;
J. Allan Cash Ltd; The Mansell Collection;
Mary Evans Picture Library;
The National Film Archive; Popperfoto Ltd.

Introduction

Check Your English consists of two Student's Books of 20 units each and a cassette for each book. The Teachers' Books include answer keys to the Student's Book exercises, notes on methodology and cassette transcripts.

Each unit has a checkpoint, language items, a consolidation section, a language summary and a test.

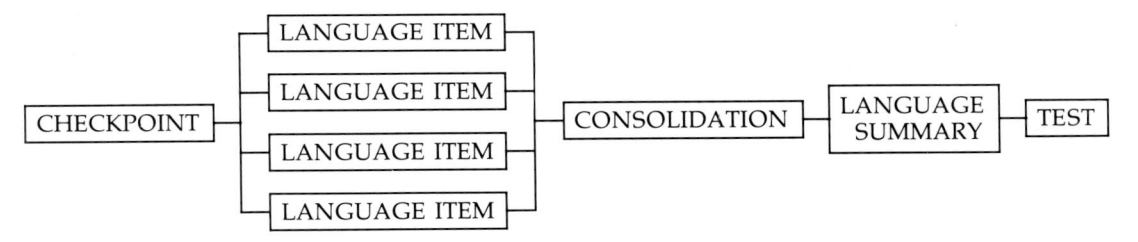

```
                    ┌─ LANGUAGE ITEM ─┐
                    ├─ LANGUAGE ITEM ─┤                   ┌─ LANGUAGE ─┐
    CHECKPOINT ─────┤                 ├── CONSOLIDATION ──┤  SUMMARY   ├── TEST
                    ├─ LANGUAGE ITEM ─┤                   └────────────┘
                    └─ LANGUAGE ITEM ─┘
```

Checkpoint – will help you check which language items you need to revise in a unit.

Language Items – give practice in those areas of language (grammar, structures, functions, etc.) that you will need in order to express yourself fluently and accurately in English.

Consolidation – gives further practice in *all* the items practised separately earlier in the unit.

Language Summary – contains grammar notes and rules on the language points covered in each unit. You will need to complete these rules to make sure that you have fully understood them. They will be useful for reference.

Test – At the end of each unit there is a test. This will show you how much you have learnt, and whether you need to look at any of the language items again.

Contents

Unit	Functional/Notional Area	Language Item	Topic	Page
1	Personal Information Information about Nature	A. Present Simple (1) States B. Present Simple (2) Habits C. Present Simple (3) General Truths	Daily Life	6
2	Likes, Dislikes and Preferences	A. Like doing B. Like to do C. Preferences	Activities	14
3	Wishes and Requests	A. Informal B. Formal C. Neutral	Eating Out	22
4	Asking for and Giving Directions	A. Imperatives B. Get C. You go ...	Towns	30
5	Describing (1) – Actions	A. Present Continuous – 'now' B. Present Continuous – Long-term Developments C. Present Continuous/Present Simple	The Seaside	38
6	Past Events Confirming Facts	A. Past Simple (1) Short Actions B. Past Simple (2) Long Actions C. Past Simple (3) Confirming Facts	Hospitals	46
7	Past Events	A. Past Simple and Past Simple Passive B. Past Simple Passive	News and History	54
8	Describing (2) – People, Things and Places	A. Describing People B. Describing Things C. Describing Places	People, Things and Places	62
9	Comparing	A. As ... as ... B. Comparatives and Superlatives C. (Not) enough/too	Transport	70
10	Rules	A. Can/can't/may B. Allowed to/not allowed to/must C. Let/don't let	Accommodation	78

Unit	Functional/Notional Area	Language Item	Topic	Page
11	Permission	A. Permission – Informal/Neutral B. Permission – Formal C. Refusing Permission	Jobs	86
12	Decisions for the Future Thinking about the Future	A. Going to B. Verb + to C. Verb/adjective + (that) + clause	Holidays	94
13	Talking about Sensations and Appearances	A. Can B. Like/as if (though) C. Seem (to)	Illness	102
14	Obligation	A. Must/have to B. Mustn't/don't have to	Foreign Travel	110
15	Advice	A. Should/ought to B. Informal Advice C. Formal Advice	Personal Problems	118
16	Describing Something in the Past	A. Past Continuous B. Past Continuous/Past Simple	Witnessing Events	126
17	Progress and Completion	A. Present Perfect Simple (Progress) B. Present Perfect Simple (Completion)	Practical Problems	134
18	Duration	A. Present Perfect Simple/Past Simple B. For/since/ago	Studying	142
19	Reason and Purpose	A. Present Simple Passive B. Eliciting Information: expressing reason and purpose	Science and Knowledge	150
20	Reporting	A. Say/tell/ask B. Tense Changes C. Pronoun Changes D. Changes to Adverbials of Time	Messages, Instructions, Reports	158

1 SUMMARY OF CONTENTS

Functional/notional areas	Personal Information Information about Nature
Language item(s)	A. Present Simple States B. Present Simple Habits C. Present Simple General Truths
Topic	Daily Life

Present Simple: States, habits and general truths

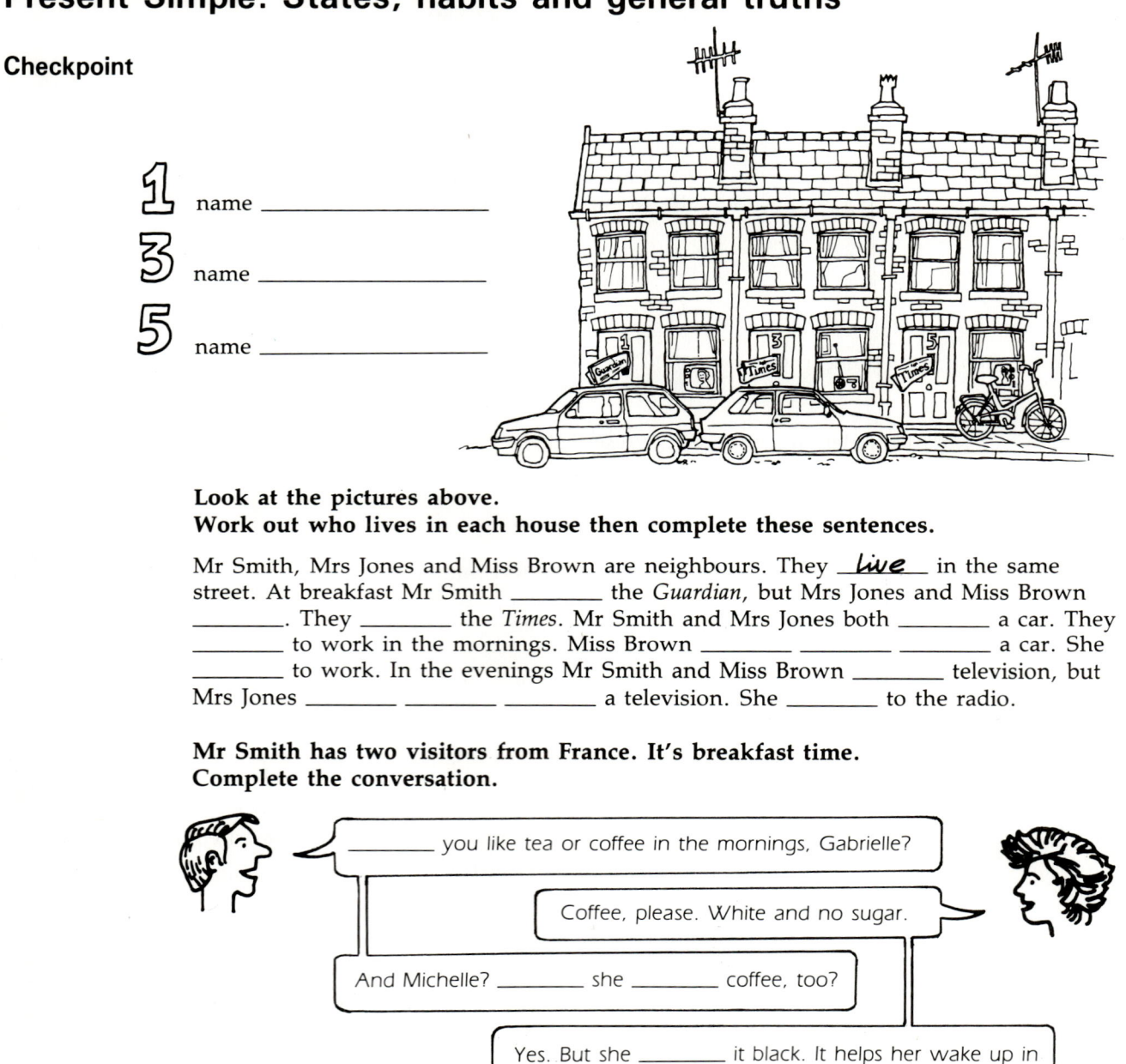

Checkpoint

1 name _____
3 name _____
5 name _____

Look at the pictures above.
Work out who lives in each house then complete these sentences.

Mr Smith, Mrs Jones and Miss Brown are neighbours. They _live_ in the same street. At breakfast Mr Smith _____ the *Guardian*, but Mrs Jones and Miss Brown _____. They _____ the *Times*. Mr Smith and Mrs Jones both _____ a car. They _____ to work in the mornings. Miss Brown _____ _____ _____ a car. She _____ to work. In the evenings Mr Smith and Miss Brown _____ television, but Mrs Jones _____ _____ _____ a television. She _____ to the radio.

Mr Smith has two visitors from France. It's breakfast time.
Complete the conversation.

_____ you like tea or coffee in the mornings, Gabrielle?

Coffee, please. White and no sugar.

And Michelle? _____ she _____ coffee, too?

Yes. But she _____ it black. It helps her wake up in the mornings!

A States

1. Listen to the interview and write down the questions the interviewer asks about the following:

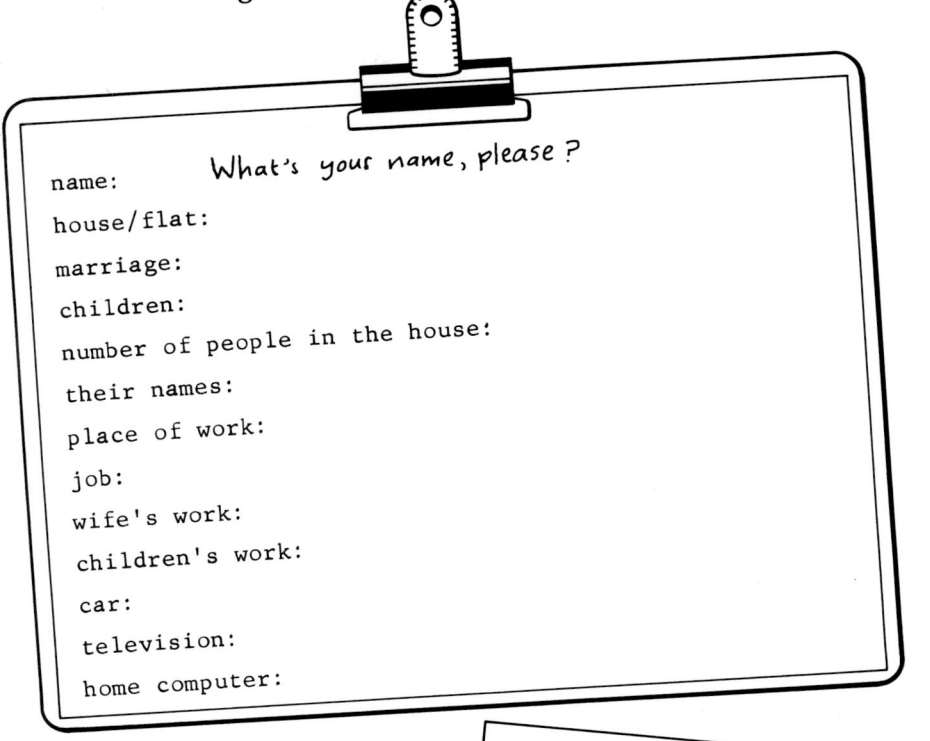

```
name:          What's your name, please?
house/flat:
marriage:
children:
number of people in the house:
their names:
place of work:
job:
wife's work:
children's work:
car:
television:
home computer:
```

2. Look at the form and listen to the interview again. The interviewer has made five mistakes. What are they? Put a circle round each mistake and correct it. One has been done for you.

MARKET RESEARCH SURVEY 65B/34X/3170085/3

Name: Robin Jackson
Residence: House ☐ Flat ☑   Marital Status: Single ☐ Married ☑
No. of children: 0 ☑ 1 ☐ 2 ☐ 3 ☐ More ☐
No. of people living in residence: 1/2 ☐ 3/4 ☐ 5/6 ☑ 7/8 ☐ more ☐
Place of work: University
Occupation: Teacher

Other inhabitants and occupations:

NAME	RELATION	OCCUPATION
Angela Jackson	wife	(lecturer)
Robert Jackson	son	at school
Richard Jackson	son	at school
Ann Jackson	daughter	at school
John Clements	father-in-law	retired

Car owner: Yes ☑ No ☐   TV owner: Yes ☐ No ☑
Home computer owner: Yes ☐ No ☑

3. Work in pairs. Ask your partner questions and fill in the form for him/her.

A: *What's your name, please?*
B: _____

4. Work in groups. Imagine you are a famous living person. The other students must ask you questions to find out who you are. You can only answer 'Yes' or 'No'.

B Habits

Mr and Mrs Jackson live in Churchill Road. Mrs Jackson works at a local school and her husband is a lecturer at the university. In the morning Mrs Jackson usually drives to work so Mr Jackson goes by bus. Look at the morning timetable for the number 67 bus.

Service 67	CHURCHILL ROAD/UNIVERSITY				
Churchill Road	0801	0811	0825	0841	0851
St Anne's Rd	0805	0815	0829	0845	0855
West St	0812	0822	0836	0852	0902
The Park	0816	0826	0840	0856	0906
South St	0819	0829	0843	0859	0909
The White Horse	0825	0835	0849	0905	0915
Gloucester Rd	0829	0839	0853	0909	0919
University	0835	0845	0859	0915	0925

1. In pairs, ask and answer questions like these about the timetable.

A: *What time does the 8.11 arrive at the university?*
B: *It gets there at _____.*

A: *When does the 8.41 get to South St?*
B: *It arrives at _____.*

2. Work in pairs. Student A look at this page; student B at page 13.

This is part of the evening bus timetable from the university. Ask each other questions to find out the missing times on each timetable, and write them in.

Service 67	UNIVERSITY/CHURCHILL ROAD			
University	1630	1650	1710	1730
Gloucester Rd	1639	1656	**1716**	1736
The White Horse		1659		
South St		1704		
The Park				1726
West St	1654		1731	
St Anne's Rd	1703		1740	
Churchill Rd	1708		1745	1805

3. Some of Mr Jackson's colleagues also catch the number 67 bus to the university. Look at both the morning and evening timetables and fill in the blanks below to find out what Mr Jackson's colleagues are saying.

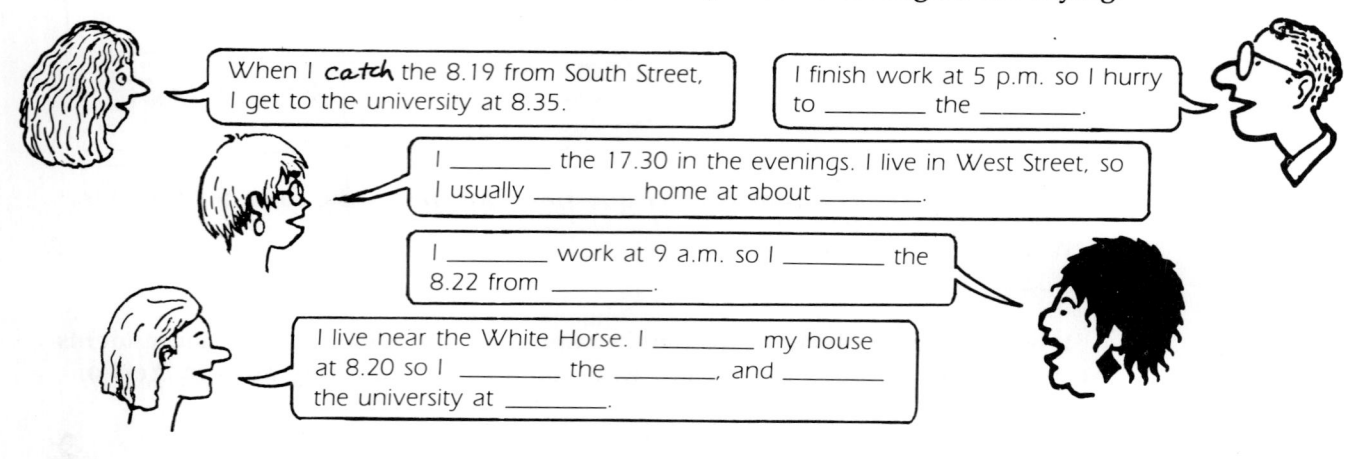

When I *catch* the 8.19 from South Street, I get to the university at 8.35.

I finish work at 5 p.m. so I hurry to _____ the _____.

I _____ the 17.30 in the evenings. I live in West Street, so I usually _____ home at about _____.

I _____ work at 9 a.m. so I _____ the 8.22 from _____.

I live near the White Horse. I _____ my house at 8.20 so I _____ the _____, and _____ the university at _____.

C General truths

Read this extract from a zoology book by Mr Jackson.

> Beavers live in N. America, Europe and Asia. They are good swimmers and live in water in the pine forests. They have large flat tails and very sharp teeth. They cut down trees with their teeth to make homes in small lakes and rivers. These homes usually have a 'dining room', a 'bedroom' and a 'living room'. They live there in families; often as many as ten beavers in one home. Beavers work very hard building and improving their homes. Sometimes in a fast river they cut down more trees and make a dam. This takes a family of beavers about ten days to build. Beavers generally eat plants, berries and tree bark. In winter they usually keep a large tree branch underwater near their home so they have enough food.

1. Look at these eight pictures and decide if each one is correct or incorrect according to the extract.

2. Match the animals with their characteristics and fill in the missing verbs.

smell   sleep   steal   live   cut   make   eat   run

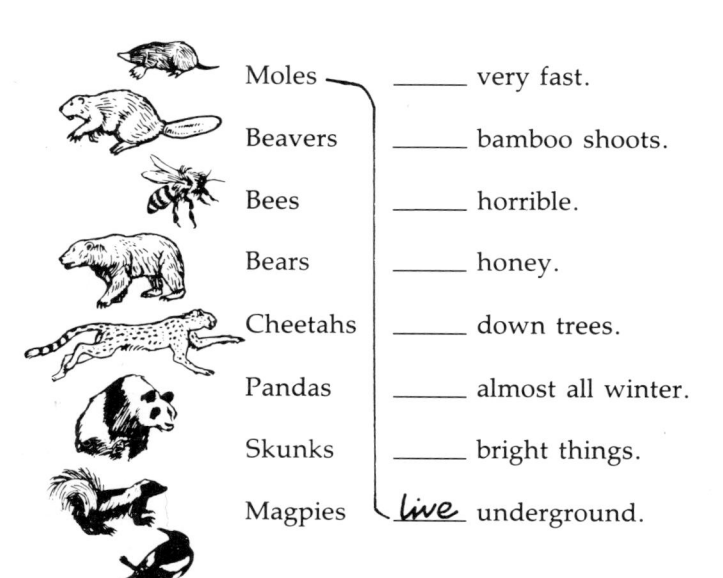

Moles — _____ very fast.
Beavers — _____ bamboo shoots.
Bees — _____ horrible.
Bears — _____ honey.
Cheetahs — _____ down trees.
Pandas — _____ almost all winter.
Skunks — _____ bright things.
Magpies — *live* underground.

3. What do you know about these animals?

Write four sentences about each animal: about where they live, what they eat, why they are interesting and any special characteristics they have. What does the shape of each animal tell you about how it lives?

Consolidation

1. Read the Safewatch advertisement and put the words in these sentences into the right order. Then decide if each sentence about Safewatch is true or false.

   a) HOUSE PROTECTS YOUR SAFEWATCH
   b) YOUR OUT FINDS SAFEWATCH ROUTINES
   c) IN SAFEWATCH THE QUESTIONNAIRES FILL MEN
   d) THEY YOUR PATROL HOUSE
   e) CARS DRIVE THEY STRANGE
   f) FOR THEY PEOPLE WATCH SUSPICIOUS
   g) CRIME STARTS STOP IT THEY BEFORE
   h) FAMILY THEY YOUR PROTECT

   SAFEWATCH

   Thieves steal thousands of pounds every year. They take televisions and videos; they take jewellery and valuables.

   Is your area safe at night?
   Is your home safe at night?
   Do you worry about burglars?

   — Safewatch guards your home.
   — Safewatch asks you about your routines and habits.
   — Safewatch asks your neighbours about their routines and habits.
   — We ask you to fill in a questionnaire.
   — Our men patrol the streets at night.
   — We look out for anything unusual.
   — We make a note of any strange cars.
   — We watch for suspicious people.
   — We stop crime before it starts.

   All this protects you, your family and your home.

   Think Safe!   **Think Safewatch!**

2. Fill in the questionnaire for yourself first. Then work in pairs and ask your partner questions so that you can fill in the second questionnaire for him or her.

   Safewatch questionnaire

   HOLIDAYS

   When you go on holiday, do you . . .
   lock all your windows?
   tell all your friends?
   cancel your newspapers?
   stop the milk delivery?
   turn off the central heating?
   tell your neighbours?
   tell everyone you meet?
   leave a key with your neighbours?
   tell the police?
   tell Safewatch?
   leave a key with Safewatch?

UNIT 1   11

3. Listen to the interview between the man from Safewatch and Mrs Jackson, and complete Mr Coleman's notes.

```
No. of people _____
No. of workers _____
ROUTINES  [AM]
Mrs J. out at _____ with _____
     back at _____ or _____.
Mr J. has _____ regular routine.
Mr J. _____ and _____ back at different times.
[PM]
Mrs J's father sometimes _____ to the pub.
Mr & Mrs J sometimes _____ to the pub.
Whole family _____
Clubs and societies _____
Note send report to regional office.
```

4. Now using your memory and the notes you have made of the interview, complete the report that Mr Coleman wrote about his meeting with Mrs Jackson.

```
Report on Jackson family, Churchill Road.
Six people  live  in the Jackson household. Mr and Mrs
Jackson both _____; their three children _____ to
school; Mrs Jackson's father _____ _____ work.
In the mornings Mrs Jackson always _____ the house
at 7.30 a.m. with the children and _____ back
between 5.00 and 5.30 p.m. Her husband, however,
_____ not always _____ and _____ back at the
same time. In the evenings there is no special routine.
Mrs Jackson's father sometimes _____ to the pub.
Mr and Mrs Jackson sometimes _____ to the pub, too.
Occasionally the whole family _____ to the cinema.
They _____ not _____ to any societies.

Interviewed by:
      G A Coleman
G.A. Coleman
```

Language Summary

Complete the summary by filling in the blanks with words from the box.

Use

cut
do
do
does
doesn't
don't
don't
drink
eat
have
jump
live
lives
own
visit

We use the Present Simple:

1. To talk about the permanent things in our lives (*States*)
   She ___lives___ in a house.
   He _____ _____ in a flat.
   _____ she _____ a car?

2. To talk about things we do regularly (*Habits*)
   _____ you _____ breakfast at 7 o'clock every day?
   They _____ usually _____ coffee.
   We _____ my parents every Sunday.

3. To talk about things that are always true (*General truths*)
   Beavers _____ down trees.
   Panda _____ _____ fish.
   _____ kangaroos _____ very high?

Form

I You We They	eat	fruit.
He She It	eats	

I You We They	don't	eat meat.
He She It	doesn't	

Do	I you we they	eat vegetables?
Does	he she it	

Yes,	I you we they	do.
	he she it	does.

No,	I you we they	don't.
	he she it	doesn't.

Test Fill in the blanks in these passages.

1. My name is Andrew Jackson. I _____ in Churchill Road, Martown. I _____ a brother and a sister. We _____ with my mum, my dad and my grandad. My mum is a teacher. She _____ history and English. My dad _____ at the university.

> MY NAME IS ANDREW JACKSON.

2. I _____ up at 7 o'clock. My dad _____ my breakfast and my mum _____ us to school in the car. In the afternoons my brother and I _____ badminton and my sister _____ hockey.

3. Yesterday at school we learned about brown bears. Brown bears _____ in forests. They usually _____ berries and roots, but sometimes they _____ meat, too. In winter these bears _____ most of the time.

Student B data for information gap exercise on page 8.

Service 67	UNIVERSITY/CHURCHILL ROAD			
University	1630	1650	1710	1730
Gloucester Rd			1716	
The White Horse	1642		1719	1739
South St	1647		1724	1744
The Park	1649	1706		1746
West St		1711		1751
St Anne's Rd		1720		1800
Churchill Rd		1725		

2 SUMMARY OF CONTENTS

Functional/notional areas	Likes, Dislikes and Preferences
Language item(s)	A. Like doing B. Like to do C. Preferences
Topic	Activities

Likes, Dislikes and Preferences

Checkpoint

This is the kitchen in Neil Jones's house. What can we tell about Neil? Complete the sentences below using words from the two boxes. Put something from box 1 in column 1 and something from box 2 in column 2. In many cases more than one answer is possible. The first two have been done for you.

1	2
He _is fond of_	_listening_ to the radio.
He _likes_	_to go_ to the dentist once a year.
He _____	_____ biscuits.
He _____	_____ up.
He _____	_____ the ashtray.
He _____	_____ mice in the kitchen.
He _____	_____ spaghetti.
He _____	_____ coffee to drinking tea.
He _____	_____ tennis.
He _____	_____ fit.
He _____	_____ golf.
He _____	_____ his clothes.
He _____	_____ eggs.

A1. Try to use all the verbs in this box.

adores
loves
hates
likes
prefers
is fond of
can't stand
doesn't mind
isn't very fond of
enjoys
doesn't like

A2. You may need to use the same form more than once.

to look	drinking
eating	keeping
to empty	to drink
washing	to play
to keep	listening
to listen	having
going	cooking
looking	to wash
to eat	to go
emptying	to have
to cook	playing

A Like doing

CHRIS DAWSON is a climber. He has led expeditions to many places including one to the Himalayas in 1986.

'I adore climbing,' he told me. 'I enjoy breathing the fresh mountain air; I like looking down on the villages far away in the valleys below; and I love standing on the top of a mountain and feeling a great sense of achievement.'

However, climbing isn't always pleasant. 'There are quite a few things I don't like,' he continued. 'I hate waking up in the morning feeling cold; I don't like eating dried food all the time; and I can't stand waiting for a saucepan of snow to melt so I can have a cup of tea.'

I also asked him about the responsibilities of leading expeditions.

'I don't mind leading expeditions,' he said. 'I always choose people who know each other, so the expeditions are quite friendly. Yes, I'm quite fond of organising the trips.'

1. **Correct the false sentences.**

   a) Chris Dawson can't stand climbing.
   b) He enjoys breathing fresh air.
   c) He doesn't like looking down on villages.
   d) He hates standing on the top of a mountain.
   e) He loves waking up in the morning feeling cold.
   f) He doesn't like eating dried food.
   g) He doesn't mind waiting for his tea.
   h) He doesn't mind leading expeditions.
   i) He hates organising the trips.

2. **Work in groups of four. Use *like, not like, enjoy, hate, not mind*, etc.**

   A: Let's go to that new Chinese restaurant.
   B: Great! I love trying new places.
   C: Okay. I don't mind trying new places.
   D: Oh no! Let's do something else. I'm not very fond of trying new places.

   Let's
   - go to that new Chinese restaurant.
   - go and see *Aliens*.
   - turn the TV on.
   - go to the tennis club.
   - go to the disco.
   - walk to the next town.
   - go to the fish and chip shop.
   - enrol on a French course.
   - go down to the beach.
   - order some fried octopus.
   - go to the British Museum.

   - new places
   - cinema
   - TV
   - tennis
   - _____
   - _____
   - _____
   - _____
   - _____
   - _____
   - _____

3. **Work in groups. Tell each other about your likes and dislikes. Talk about:**

   - your hobbies
   - sport
   - restaurants
   - books
   - films
   - music

B Like to do

1. Listen to the conversation between Linda Platt and the travel agent and answer these questions.

a) Where does Linda like to stay on holiday?
b) What does she like to do in the evenings?

2. The travel agent has three holidays left. Work in pairs and decide which holiday you would recommend to Linda and why.

CAMP EUROPA
- marvellous, well-equipped camp site
- on-site restaurant and cafe
- 400 m from fantastic beach
- nearby nightly discotheque
- free watersports
- activity days—full of fun and games
- frequent buses to town centre
- TV room

Club Atlantico
Stay in our fabulous beachside club
Have your own chalet on a fantastic white sand beach
Free waterskiing and windsurfing
Nightly activities—discos, concerts, parties
Swimming pool
Buses to town three times a day
Young friendly atmosphere
Excellent food

Teens and Twenties
– 2-star seaside hotel
– beautiful beaches nearby
– plenty of watersports available
– discos every night
– young, friendly atmosphere
– superb hotel restaurant
– day trips to places of interest

3. Work in pairs. Complete these sentences using *like to*.

a) I want to keep fit and healthy. I don't travel by bus. I *like to walk everywhere*.
b) I think it's important for people to have a hobby, so in the evenings and at the weekend I _____.
c) I work very hard at my job so on holiday I _____.
d) White bread isn't very good for you, that's why I _____.
e) I only have a sandwich for lunch so in the evening I _____.
f) I hate having my teeth filled so I _____.

4. Work in groups. Tell each other what you like to do:

- when you go away on holiday.
- at weekends.
- in the evenings.

C Preferences

Steven Spielberg first became famous as a film director. He directed films such as *Close Encounters of the Third Kind* and *Jaws*. However, he doesn't like telling actors what to do, so now he prefers producing films to directing them. In fact, he rarely directs a film at all nowadays.

Warren Beatty, on the other hand, first became famous as an actor in films such as *Bonnie and Clyde* and *Shampoo*. Although he still appears on screen, he now prefers to direct films rather than act in them.

1. Work in pairs. Put the words in the right order to make true sentences.

   a) SPIELBERG PRODUCING DIRECTING PREFERS FILMS THEM TO
   b) FILMS WHAT ACTORS PRODUCING DO TELLING SPIELBERG TO TO PREFERS
   c) BEATTY ON TO THAN FILMS SCREEN PREFERS APPEAR DIRECT RATHER
   d) PREFERS TO ACT BEATTY RATHER DIRECT THAN

2. Work in pairs. Write down what these people are saying.

   I prefer *swimming to playing tennis.*
   I prefer *to swim rather than play tennis.*

3. Work in groups. Which do you prefer? Ask the other members of your group and find out why.

   Example: *Do you prefer cooking your own food or eating in a restaurant?*

   Ask about:
   - flying/travelling by train
   - having a well-paid boring job/having a badly-paid interesting job
   - eating at home/having a picnic
   - going to the cinema/watching a film on TV
   - going to a concert/listening to a record

Consolidation

1. Listen to Ann's interview with a pop star, Barry Cloud. Before the interview, Ann wrote down five questions she wanted to ask. Then during the interview she made notes about Barry's answers. Listen to the interview once and complete the questions. Listen to the interview again and complete her notes.

1. What ___ ___ ___ ___ ___ ___ ?
   Doesn't like ___ ___ discos, parties, leading a ___ life. Likes to ___ ___ ___ ___ and ___ an interesting ___ .

2. How ___ ___ ___ ___ spend your mornings?
   ___ breakfast.
   Likes to ___ ___ ___ ___ .

3. How ___ ___ ___ ?
   Loves ___ ___ .
   Enjoys sitting ___ ___ ___ ___ , relaxing, ___ .

4. What ___ ___ ___ ___ ___ work?
   Works for ___ ___ a year.
   Prefers concert tours to ___ .
   Prefers ___ new people.

5. Is there anything that you really ___ ___ ___ ___ ?
   Prefers touring ___ Europe.
   Last year ___ ___ concerts in ___ ___ .
   Loved traditional songs and the dancing was ___ .
   Not fond of ___ ___ concerts in ___ days.

2. After her interview with Barry, Ann found an article about him in another newspaper. She was pleased to see that the other journalist had made several mistakes. Find the mistakes (there are six), put a circle round them, and correct them. The first has been done for you.

STARFILE

wild

BARRY CLOUD is an unusual pop star. He doesn't like staying out late at night, going to parties and discos, and leading a ~~quiet~~ life. He likes to go to bed early and read an interesting magazine. Then in the morning after a quick breakfast of a cup of coffee and a piece of toast, he likes to go for a jog along the road in front of his house. In the afternoons Barry loves playing tennis with some of his friends or else he enjoys sitting by the swimming pool at the tennis club, chatting and relaxing. For seven months each year he makes records and goes on concert tours. He says he prefers going on tours and meeting new people to sitting in recording studios with the same old faces. He also prefers to tour in exotic countries rather than stay in England. Last year he played six concerts in South Africa where he loved watching the local singing and dancing. 'The concerts were hard work though,' he said. 'I'm not very fond of playing six concerts in seven days. Still, we can't have fun all the time I suppose.' Life doesn't seem too bad for Barry Cloud!

3. Roleplay: Work in pairs.

A:
You are famous pop stars and you are going to be interviewed for the *Starfile* column. Decide on a name. Think what questions the interviewer might ask. Prepare your answers.

B:
You are going to interview a famous pop star for the *Starfile* column. Decide what questions to ask. Prepare what you will say.

Now form new pairs (one A, one B) and act out the interview. Make notes. When you have finished, change roles (A becomes B, B becomes A) and after some preparation, have more interviews.

4. Now write your own *Starfile* column about the person you interviewed.

Language Summary

Complete the summary by filling the blanks with words and phrases from the boxes on the right.

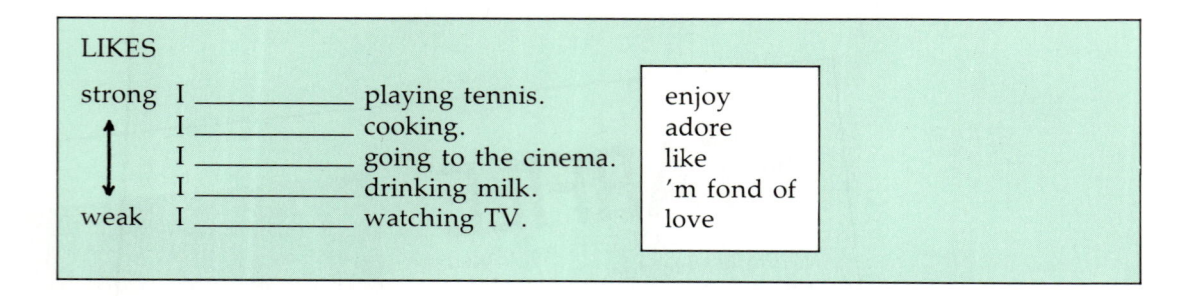

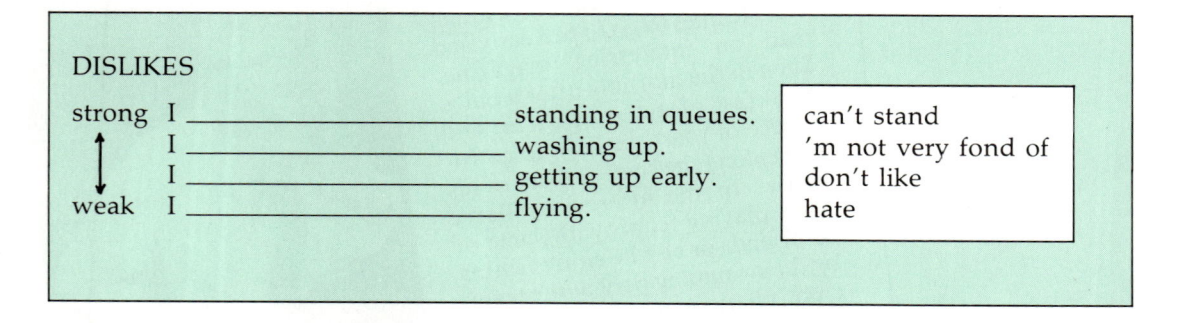

LIKES

strong I _____ playing tennis.
       I _____ cooking.
       I _____ going to the cinema.
       I _____ drinking milk.
weak I _____ watching TV.

enjoy
adore
like
'm fond of
love

DISLIKES

strong I _____ standing in queues.
       I _____ washing up.
       I _____ getting up early.
weak I _____ flying.

can't stand
'm not very fond of
don't like
hate

NO PREFERENCE

I don't mind travelling by bus.

LIKE TO DO or LIKE DOING

I like _____ = I enjoy jogging.
I like _____ = I think it's a good idea to jog. I like to be healthy.

to jog
jogging

PREFERENCE

Do you prefer { cooking at home to eating in a restaurant?
                { to cook at home rather than (to) eat in a restaurant?

I prefer cooking at home to eating in a restaurant.
I prefer to cook at home rather than eat in a restaurant.
I prefer { to cook at home.
        { cooking at home.

Test

Write sentences using *like, hate, love,* etc.

Example: *Michael never eats mushrooms.*
He _____

1. Edna thinks it's a good idea to eat brown bread all the time.
   She _____

2. Elsie does the washing up once a week.
   She _____

3. Albert doesn't like getting up early, but he doesn't hate it either.
   _____

4. Mark's very lazy.
   _____

5. John and Jean always drink orange juice if they can. Otherwise they have lemonade.
   _____

6. Jenny drinks milk for breakfast every day.
   _____

7. Jackie doesn't go to her English lessons if she can think of something better to do.
   _____

8. Whenever Mary flies, she gets very frightened.
   _____

9. Kevin trains every Tuesday, cleans his boots every Friday, and plays football every Saturday.
   _____

10. Edwina never eats fruit. She never eats eggs, either.
    _____

3

SUMMARY OF CONTENTS

Functional/notional areas	Wishes and Requests
Language item(s)	A. Informal B. Formal C. Neutral
Topic	Eating Out

Wishes and Requests

Checkpoint   What would you say in these situations?

1. You are ordering a meal in a restaurant. You want steak and chips.
2. You are in your boss's office and he offers you tea or coffee. You want coffee.
3. Your friend asks you where you want to go for a meal. You want to go to the new Indian restaurant.
4. You are having tea with your boyfriend's/girlfriend's parents for the first time. You want some sugar in your tea.
5. You are having dinner at a friend's house. He offers you cheese or dessert. You want cheese.
6. You are discussing where to go on holiday with your best friend. You really want to go to France.
7. You are having dinner at your boss's house. You want someone to pass the salt.
8. You are buying tickets for the theatre. You want two seats in the stalls.
9. You are buying an ice-cream. The assistant asks what flavour you want. You want a strawberry one.

A Informal

1. Listen to the conversation between three people in a restaurant. What does everyone want to eat? Fill in the box below.

Maggie	Liz	Charles

2. Listen to the conversation again and write down the different ways in which the guests say what they want.

3. Work in groups. One person is a waiter, the others are guests at the restaurant. The guests must look at the menu below and decide what they want to eat. Then they must order from the waiter. The waiter should take down the order and then work out the bill.

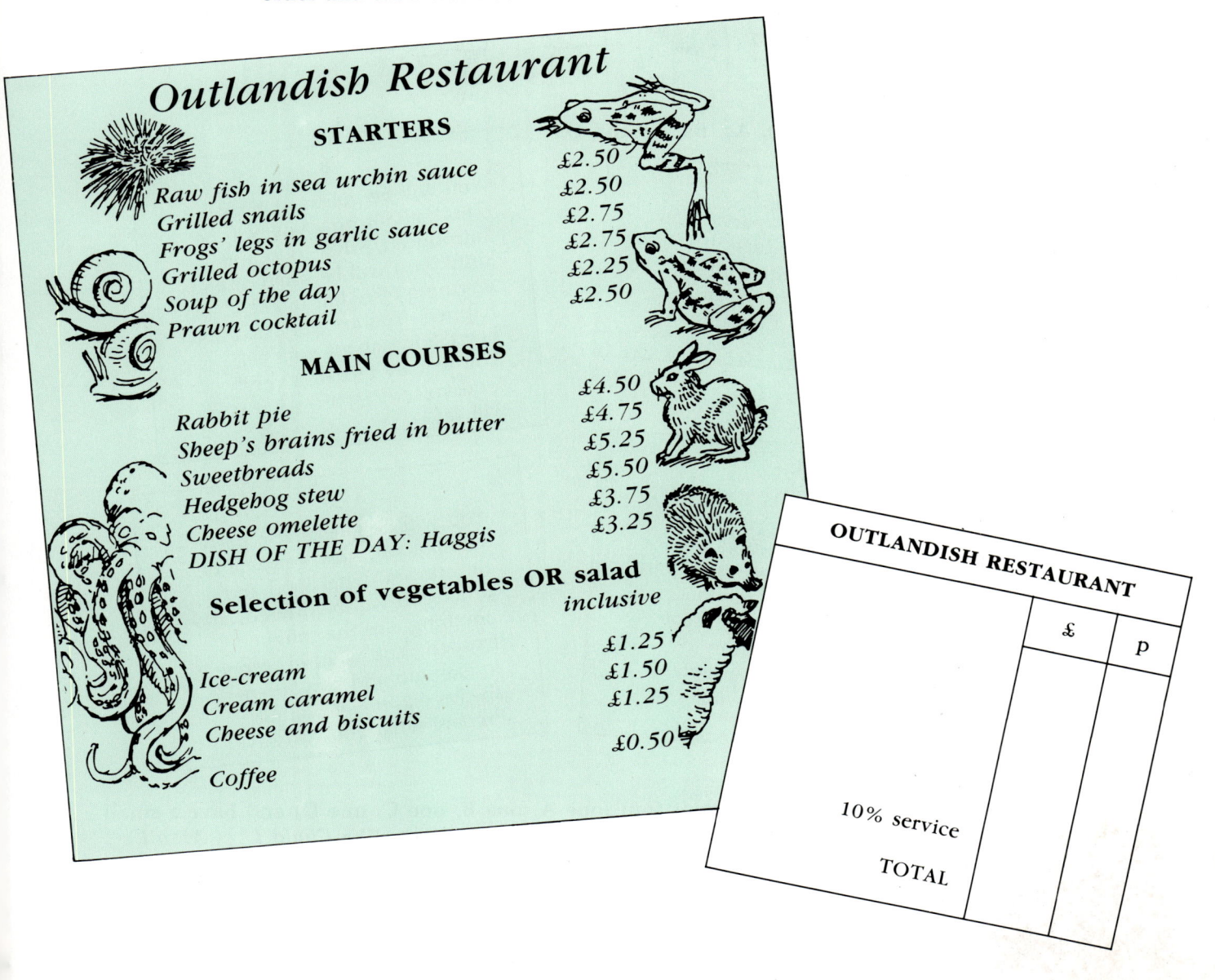

Outlandish Restaurant

STARTERS

Raw fish in sea urchin sauce — £2.50
Grilled snails — £2.50
Frogs' legs in garlic sauce — £2.75
Grilled octopus — £2.75
Soup of the day — £2.25
Prawn cocktail — £2.50

MAIN COURSES

Rabbit pie — £4.50
Sheep's brains fried in butter — £4.75
Sweetbreads — £5.25
Hedgehog stew — £5.50
Cheese omelette — £3.75
DISH OF THE DAY: Haggis — £3.25

Selection of vegetables OR salad — inclusive

Ice-cream — £1.25
Cream caramel — £1.50
Cheese and biscuits — £1.25
Coffee — £0.50

OUTLANDISH RESTAURANT

	£	P
10% service		
TOTAL		

B Formal

1. Listen to the recording of the party and complete the sentences below.

   a) _____ I _____ another drink, please?
   b) _____ I _____ sit down for a moment?
   c) Yes. I'd _____ _____ like _____ meet your husband.
   d) Oh yes! I'd _____ _____ _____ to try one.
   e) Do _____ _____ I _____ open the window?

2. Now look at the picture. Which person is saying which sentence? Match each speech bubble with the appropriate sentence from a) to e) in 1 above.

3. Work in groups, As, Bs, Cs and Ds.

   A
   You are hosts at a party. You are going to introduce the guests to each other, offer them food and drink, and look after them. Prepare what you will say.

   B
   You will be guests at a party. Think about how you will be introduced, what food and drink you will be offered, and anything else that might happen. You are very rich and like talking about yourself. You usually talk in a very loud voice. Prepare what you will say.

   C
   You will be guests at a party. Think about how you will be introduced, what food and drink you will be offered, and anything else that might happen. You are very talkative. You enjoy talking to people about other people at the party. Prepare what you will say.

   D
   You will be guests at a party. Think about how you will be introduced, what food and drink you will be offered, and anything else that might happen. You want everyone to like you and so you are always extremely polite. Prepare what you will say.

   Now work in new groups of four (one A, one B, one C, one D) and have a small party. Try to keep the conversation going. Use phrases like *Could I .../May I .../I'd very much like .../*etc.

C Neutral

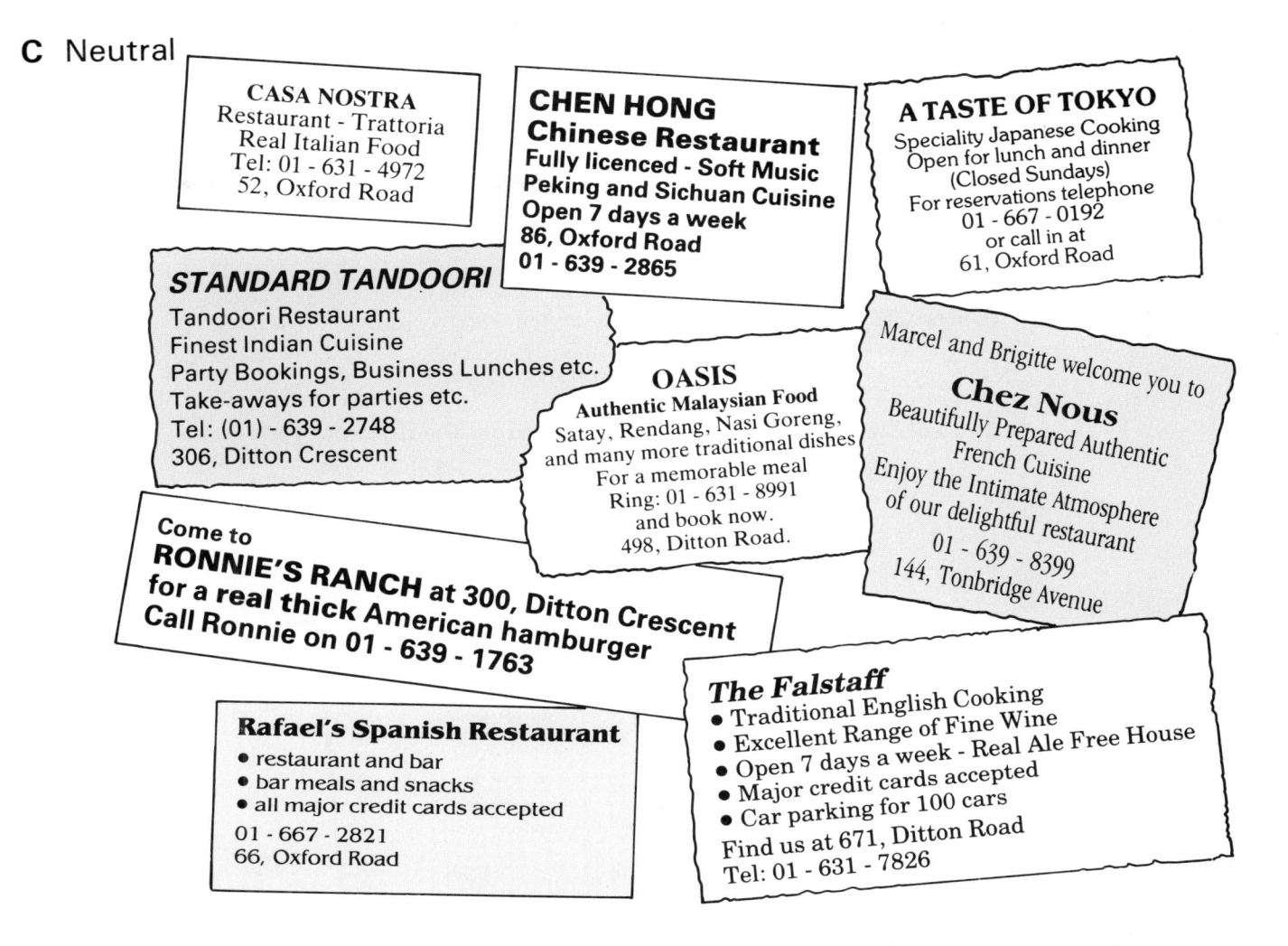

CASA NOSTRA
Restaurant - Trattoria
Real Italian Food
Tel: 01 - 631 - 4972
52, Oxford Road

CHEN HONG
Chinese Restaurant
Fully licenced - Soft Music
Peking and Sichuan Cuisine
Open 7 days a week
86, Oxford Road
01 - 639 - 2865

A TASTE OF TOKYO
Speciality Japanese Cooking
Open for lunch and dinner
(Closed Sundays)
For reservations telephone
01 - 667 - 0192
or call in at
61, Oxford Road

STANDARD TANDOORI
Tandoori Restaurant
Finest Indian Cuisine
Party Bookings, Business Lunches etc.
Take-aways for parties etc.
Tel: (01) - 639 - 2748
306, Ditton Crescent

OASIS
Authentic Malaysian Food
Satay, Rendang, Nasi Goreng,
and many more traditional dishes
For a memorable meal
Ring: 01 - 631 - 8991
and book now.
498, Ditton Road.

Marcel and Brigitte welcome you to
Chez Nous
Beautifully Prepared Authentic
French Cuisine
Enjoy the Intimate Atmosphere
of our delightful restaurant
01 - 639 - 8399
144, Tonbridge Avenue

Come to
RONNIE'S RANCH at 300, Ditton Crescent
for a real thick American hamburger
Call Ronnie on 01 - 639 - 1763

Rafael's Spanish Restaurant
- restaurant and bar
- bar meals and snacks
- all major credit cards accepted
01 - 667 - 2821
66, Oxford Road

The Falstaff
- Traditional English Cooking
- Excellent Range of Fine Wine
- Open 7 days a week - Real Ale Free House
- Major credit cards accepted
- Car parking for 100 cars
Find us at 671, Ditton Road
Tel: 01 - 631 - 7826

1. Listen to the discussion between the four people deciding where to go for lunch and fill in the table below.

NAME	WANTS TO GO	DOESN'T WANT TO GO
Mrs Green		
Mr Dickinson		
Mrs Starling		
Mr Higgins		

2. How do the different people on the cassette say they want to:

- suggest they all go out for lunch?
- go to the Japanese restaurant?
- have a look at the list?
- eat something continental?
- go to the traditional English restaurant?
- eat some traditional English food?

3. Work in pairs. Using the advertisements and the words and phrases in 2, decide where you would like to go for a meal. When you have finished, tell the class what you have decided.

4. Work in groups of four. Decide what you would like to do together after the lesson. When you have finished, tell the class what you decided.

Consolidation

1. Listen to the conversation between Gillian, Paul and Gillian's father, then choose the best ending for each of these sentences:

Gillian's father and mother want (a) to go to *Home Cooking*.
(b) a big party.
(c) a small party.

Gillian would like (a) to have about 70 or 80 guests.
(b) to go to *The Gourmet*.
(c) to have about 25 guests.

Paul would like (a) to go to *The Crab Restaurant*.
(b) a big party.
(c) to eat Chicken Kiev.

2. Look at these three wedding menus from the different restaurants.

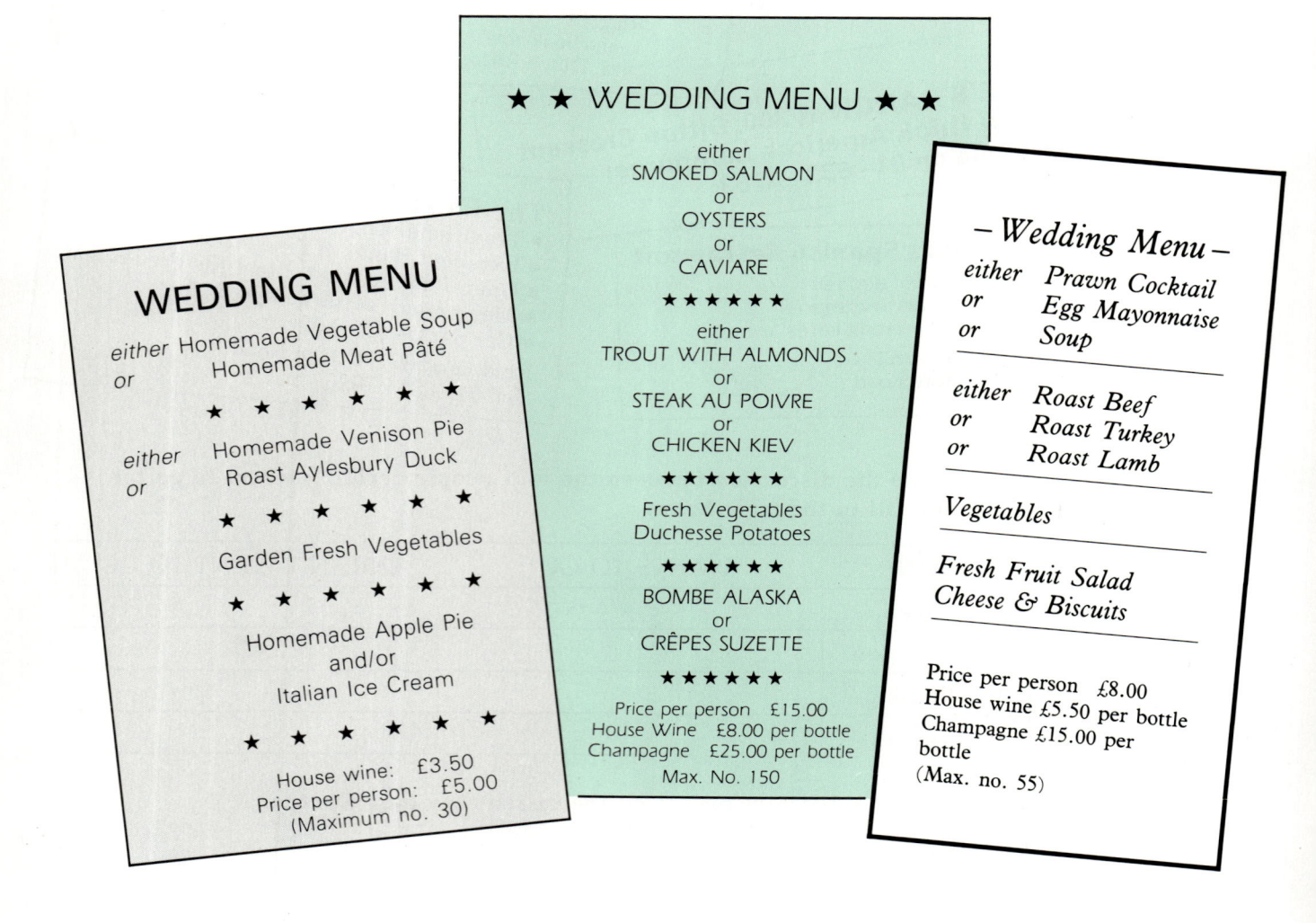

WEDDING MENU

either Homemade Vegetable Soup
or Homemade Meat Pâté

★ ★ ★ ★ ★ ★

either Homemade Venison Pie
or Roast Aylesbury Duck

★ ★ ★ ★ ★ ★

Garden Fresh Vegetables

★ ★ ★ ★ ★ ★

Homemade Apple Pie
and/or
Italian Ice Cream

★ ★ ★ ★ ★ ★

House wine: £3.50
Price per person: £5.00
(Maximum no. 30)

★ ★ WEDDING MENU ★ ★

either
SMOKED SALMON
or
OYSTERS
or
CAVIARE

★ ★ ★ ★ ★ ★

either
TROUT WITH ALMONDS
or
STEAK AU POIVRE
or
CHICKEN KIEV

★ ★ ★ ★ ★ ★

Fresh Vegetables
Duchesse Potatoes

★ ★ ★ ★ ★ ★

BOMBE ALASKA
or
CRÊPES SUZETTE

★ ★ ★ ★ ★ ★

Price per person £15.00
House Wine £8.00 per bottle
Champagne £25.00 per bottle
Max. No. 150

— Wedding Menu —

either Prawn Cocktail
or   Egg Mayonnaise
or   Soup

either Roast Beef
or   Roast Turkey
or   Roast Lamb

Vegetables

Fresh Fruit Salad
Cheese & Biscuits

Price per person £8.00
House wine £5.50 per bottle
Champagne £15.00 per bottle
(Max. no. 55)

3. Roleplay: Work in pairs, As, Bs and Cs.

Pair A
You are Gillian's father and mother. You would like to have the wedding reception at The Gourmet restaurant. You don't want to spoil Gillian's wedding but you are paying for the reception. Prepare what you will say to try and persuade her.

Pair B
You are Gillian. You would like a small party at Home Cooking. You don't want to make your parents angry but it is *your* wedding day. Prepare what you will say to try and persuade them.

Pair C
You are Paul. You think The Crab Restaurant is the best solution. You don't want to argue with your fiancée or her parents, but you are sure they would be happier going to The Crab. Prepare what you will say to try and persuade them.

Now work together in threes (one A, one B, one C) and decide where to go. When you have agreed on a restaurant, decide how many people you will invite and what food you will have.

4. When you have decided where to go and what to eat, complete the letter.

```
                                          47 Marchmont Avenue
                                          Newcastle-Upon-Tyne
                                          17th June 1985
Dear Sir/Madam,

My daughter is getting married on the 25th August
and I_____to make a booking at your restaurant
for that day. I_____to book for_____guests.
We have looked at your menu and we_____to order
_____as a starter,_____as a
main course and_____for dessert.
Perhaps we could discuss the arrangements for wine later.
We look forward to hearing from you.
Yours faithfully,
G. Stevens
```

Language Summary

Complete the summary of wishes and requests by filling the blanks on the left with the words in the boxes on the right. You can use some of the words more than once.

INFORMAL	
I _____ to go to the Indian restaurant. I'd _____ some potatoes. I'd _____ to come to your place on Friday. I (don't) _____ spaghetti. I'll _____ a beer. I really _____ going to Greece this summer.	have love want fancy

NEUTRAL	
_____ I _____ a gin and tonic? _____ I open the window? I'd _____ a fillet steak. I'd _____ _____ have a day off on Friday. _____ you move along the platform, please?	could like to have

FORMAL	
_____ I _____ the fish? _____ I _____ have some ice? _____ you _____ I _____ have some ice-cream? _____ I _____ close the door? _____ you _____ I _____ make a suggestion? I'd very much _____ _____ try the new Chinese restaurant. _____ you _____ pass the marmalade, please?	to have may like think do to possibly could

Test

Look at the situations below. How appropriate are the requests in italics? Mark them (a), (b), or (c) according to what you think.

1. You are in a restaurant and you want a cup of coffee. You say to the waiter: *I'd very much like a cup of coffee.*
   (a) correct   (b) too formal   (c) rude

2. You are in the boss's office on your first day in a new job. He offers you a drink. You say: *I'll have a beer.*
   (a) too casual   (b) too formal   (c) correct

3. Your friend offers you a drink in a bar one afternoon. You say: *Could I possibly have a fresh orange juice?*
   (a) too friendly   (b) correct   (c) too formal

4. You are having dinner at the home of a very formal business colleague who is senior to you and twenty years older. His wife offers you tea or coffee.
   You say: *I fancy a cup of coffee.*
   (a) too casual   (b) correct   (c) too polite

5. You have met your girlfriend's/boyfriend's parents for the first time at their house. It's a very hot day. You say: *Could I open the window?*
   (a) too casual   (b) correct   (c) rude

6. You go into a shop and ask the assistant: *Could I possibly have a box of chocolates?*
   (a) not polite enough   (b) too polite   (c) correct

7. You are in a travel agent's buying two tickets to Hong Kong. You say: *I'd like two tickets to Hong Kong, please.*
   (a) correct   (b) not friendly enough   (c) not formal enough

8. You are in a bank and want to write a cheque but your pen is empty. You ask the person next to you: *Do you think I could borrow your pen?*
   (a) not formal enough   (b) too casual   (c) correct

4 SUMMARY OF CONTENTS

Functional/notional areas	Asking for and Giving Directions
Language item(s)	A. Imperatives B. Get C. You go ...
Topic	Towns

Asking for and Giving Directions

Checkpoint

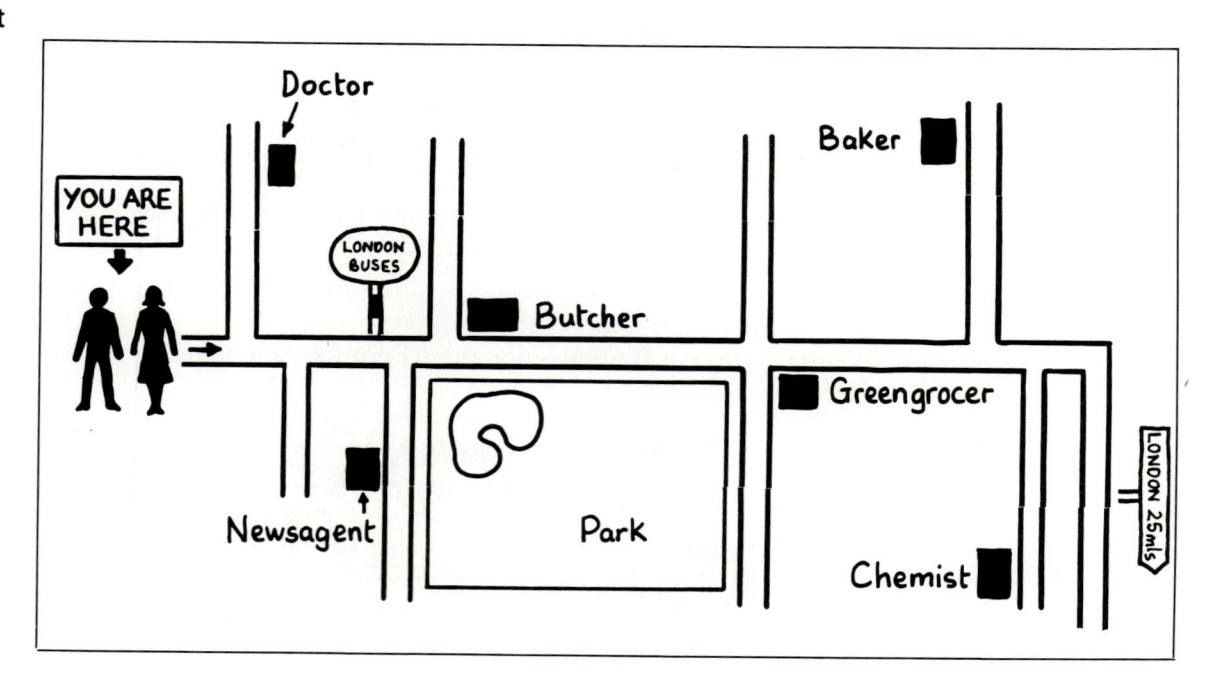

Look at the map above. Ask and give directions to the following places:

(doctor's)   A (ask): _____
               B (give): _____

(baker's)   A: _____
               B: _____

(greengrocer's) A: _____
                B: _____

(chemist's)   A: _____
               B: _____

(newsagent's) A: _____
               B: _____

(butcher's)   A: _____
               B: _____

(London)   A: _____
               B: _____

A Imperatives

1. Read the three notes below. Look at the map, then answer the questions.

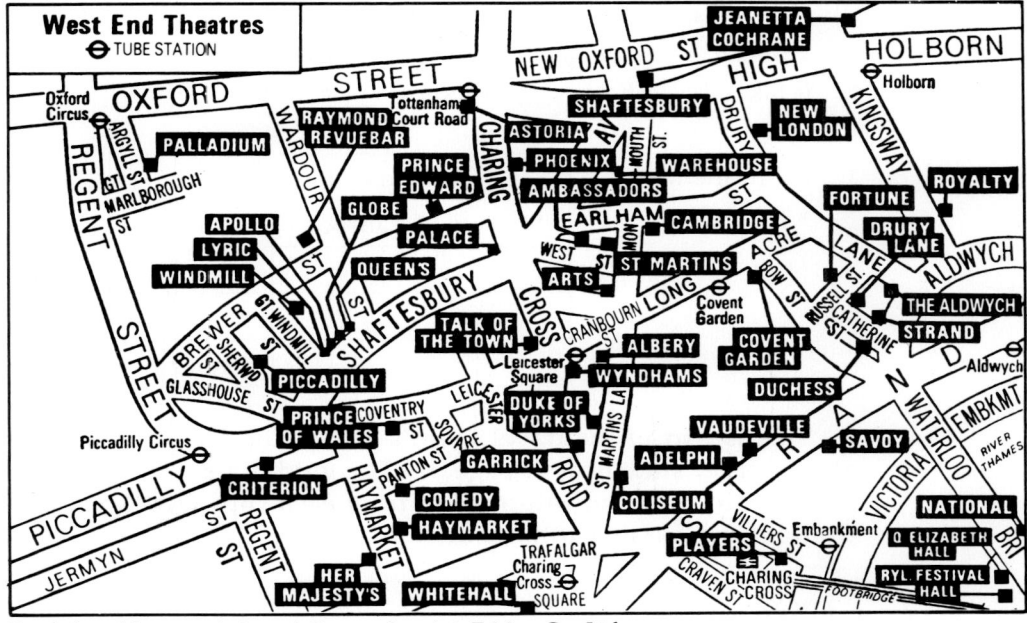

> Dick,
> The play starts at 8.00. Go to Holborn tube station. Turn left and walk along Kingsway. Turn right into the Aldwych and take the second turning right into Catherine Street. The theatre is on your left. Don't be late!
> Anna

> Mark,
> The play starts at 8.30. Go to Covent Garden tube station. Turn right and walk along Long Acre. Take the first turning right into Bow Street. Then take the first turning left into Russell St. The theatre is on your left. Meet you outside,
> Bill

> Julie,
> The play starts at 8.15. Go to Leicester Square tube station. Turn right and go along Cranbourn Street. Take the second turning left into Monmouth St. The theatre is on the corner of West St. and Monmouth St. Meet you there at about 7.45.
> Sue

a) Which theatre are Bill and Mark going to?
b) Which theatre are Julie and Sue going to?
c) Which theatre are Dick and Anna going to?

2. In pairs, look at the map and take it in turns to find the nearest tube station and give your partner directions to the following theatres:

The Cambridge	The Vaudeville	The Palace
The Ambassadors	The Prince Edward	The Windmill

3. Work in pairs. Choose a theatre and write a note telling another pair how to get there. Don't mention the name of the theatre. Give your note to the other pair and see if they can tell you which theatre you are meeting at.

B Get

1. **Listen to the two conversations in a travel agent's and do the exercises below.**

   a) Tick (✓) the correct answers.
   You can get to Singapore ☐ by boat ☐ by plane
   It takes ☐ 8 hours ☐ 18 hours ☐ 80 hours

   b) Fill in the table.

London to Edinburgh	
Method of transport	Time
	9 hours
	4½ hours
	1 hour

2. This is part of the travel agent's Travel Guide. Work in pairs. Student A look at this page; student B at page 37. The guides are almost the same but the printer has left out different information from each copy. Ask each other questions to find out the missing information.

FROM LONDON TO	BY BOAT & COACH	BY BOAT & TRAIN	BY PLANE
New York	no service	no service	7 hours
Johannesburg			
Rio de Janeiro			
Tokyo	no service	no service	17½ hours
Sydney			
Paris	11 hours	7 hours	1 hour
Amsterdam			
Stockholm			
Rome	no service	26 hours	2½ hours
Athens	no service	28 hours	3½ hours

   Example: A: *How can we get to New York?*
   B: *Well, we can go by plane.*
   A: *How long does that take?*
   B: *About 7 hours.*
   A: *Can we get there by boat too?*
   B: *No, I don't think so.*

3. Write down the names of five towns or cities in the country you are in. Work in pairs. Ask your partner how you can get to them and how long it takes. Find out about the various methods of transport – bus, coach, plane, train, etc.

4. Write down the names of five important places in the town you are in. Work in pairs. Ask your partner how you can get to them and how long it takes. Find out about the various methods of transport – bus, taxi, tube, bicycle, etc.

C You go . . .

1. Look carefully at the map. Find the Tourist Information Office. Listen to the two conversations that took place in the Tourist Information Office. Where are the two people going?

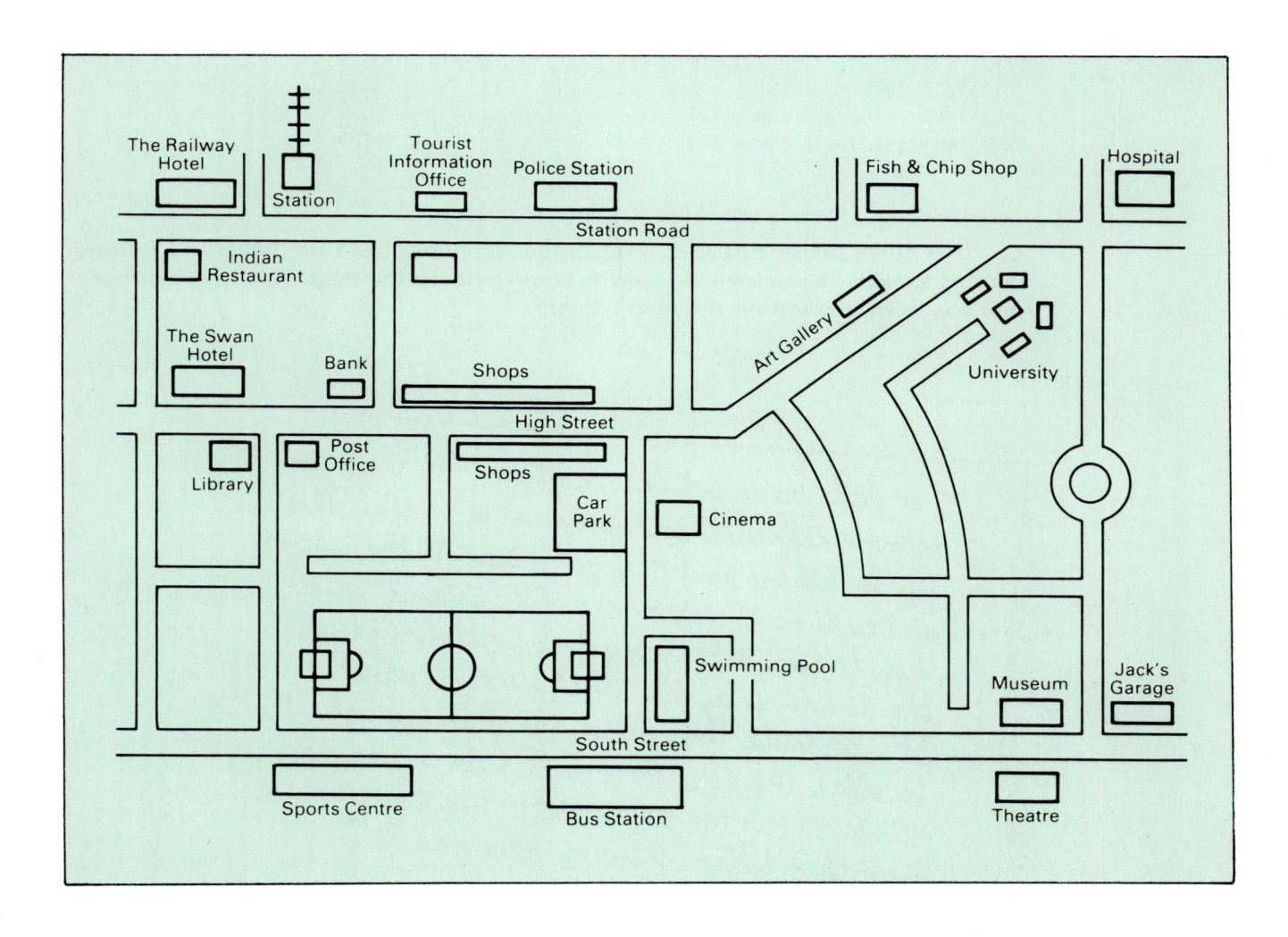

2. Work in pairs. A is a tourist; B works in the Tourist Information Office.

Example: A: *Excuse me. Could you tell me* { *where the hospital is, please?* / *how to get to the hospital, please?*

B: *Certainly. You go out of here . . .*

Ask about:
- the hospital
- the bus station
- the university
- the bank
- the museum
- the theatre etc

3. Work in pairs. Ask each other about the town you are in now. Ask about:
- the nearest bank
- the nearest garage
- the nearest telephone box
- the nearest restaurant
- the nearest swimming pool
- your flat/house

Consolidation

1. Your rich grandfather, Aristotle, has just died. You were his favourite grandchild. You are very surprised because he did not leave you any money in his will. He only left you a cassette. You go back to your house and play the cassette. Listen to the cassette, look at the map on page 35 and answer these questions:

a) Why didn't Grandad Ari leave you any money in his will?
b) Where do you start your journey?
c) Where do you go to?
d) Who do you speak to?
e) What does the manager give you?

2. These three pieces of paper were in the envelope. Read the letter and follow the instructions. Use a pencil to mark your route on the map. The first instruction has been marked on the map for you.

> I'm glad you've got the envelope. The next part is more difficult and you must be careful. First fly to Athens and then get a boat to the island of Drachmos. There's a map of the island with this letter. When you get to Drachmos follow the directions on the other piece of paper. It's possible that one of the family might try to steal the directions so I have mixed them up. YOU MUST PUT THE DIRECTIONS IN THE RIGHT ORDER. Burn this letter when you have read it.
>
> Good luck,
> Grandad Ari

DRACHMOS

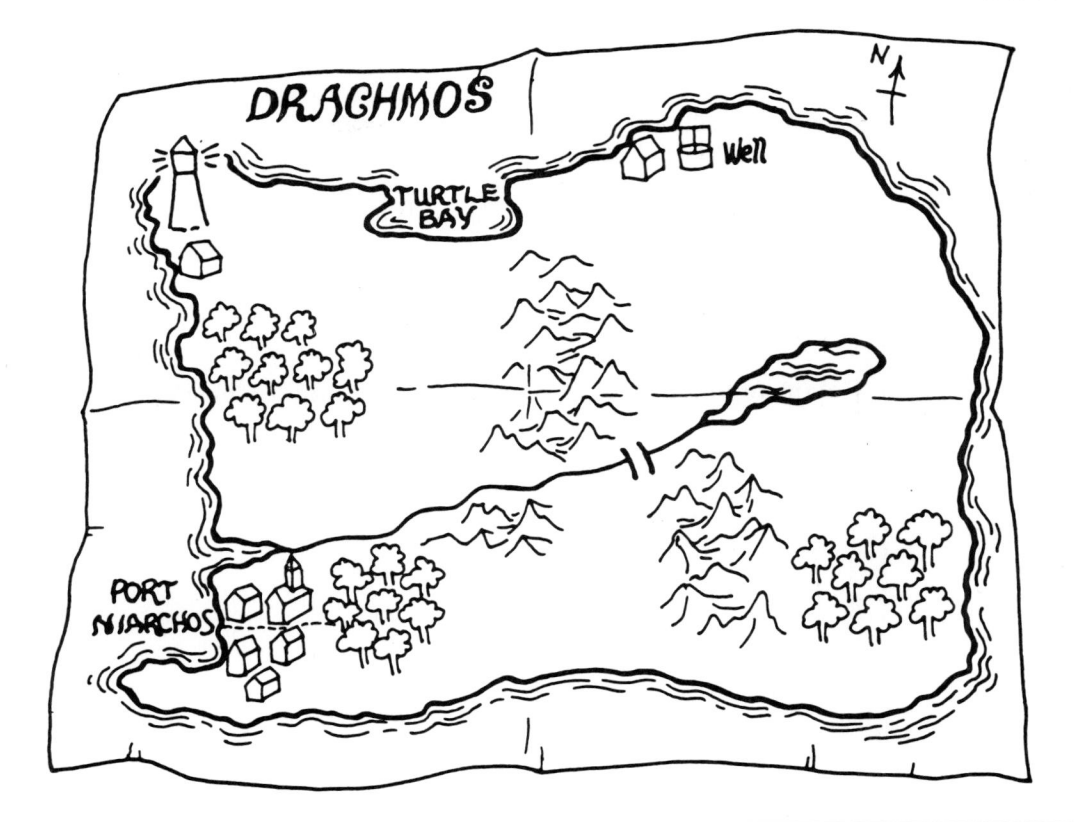

```
*   When you get to the coast, there is a well and a small house.
*   Next turn right and walk along the river.
*   Continue straight along the path until you get to the mountains.
*   After that turn left and go north until you cross the river.
1 * First go east from Port Niarchos and walk through the forest.
*   When you get to the lake turn left and walk north.
*   Spend the night there - you can drink the water from the well.
*   Go to the top of the lighthouse and look for a red box.
*   Walk round Turtle Bay.
*   In the morning walk west along the coast.
*   Then walk west again until you get to the lighthouse.
```

3. In the red box you find this message. What does it mean?

```
IMXW EAGFT MXAZS FTQ OAMEF.  FTQ FDQMEGDQ
UE UZ FTQ AXP TAGEQ.

WALK SOUTH ..... ... ..... ... .........
.. .. ... ... .....
```

UNIT 4 35

Language Summary

ASKING DIRECTIONS

Could you tell me where the station is, please?
Could you tell me how to get to the cinema, please?
Could you tell me how I get to the museum, please?
Could you tell me how I can get to Winchester, please?

GIVING DIRECTIONS

Complete this part of the summary by filling the blanks with words from the box.

Take the $\begin{cases} \text{first} \\ \text{second} \\ \text{third} \end{cases}$ _____ on the $\begin{cases} \text{left.} \\ \text{right.} \end{cases}$

Walk _____
Go _____ Exeter Street.

Turn _____
_____ into Bowes St.

*You go straight along the road _____ you $\begin{cases} \text{get to} \\ \text{reach} \end{cases}$ the bridge.

You _____ past the bus station.

You can $\begin{cases} \text{get a plane.} \\ \text{fly.} \end{cases}$

You can $\begin{cases} \text{get a bus.} \\ \text{take a boat.} \\ \text{go by train.} \end{cases}$

It's $\begin{cases} \text{on your left.} \\ \text{on your right.} \\ \text{opposite the bookshop.} \end{cases}$

| right |
| go |
| left |
| across |
| turning |
| along |
| until |

*If 'you' comes before the imperative, it makes the directions sound more friendly and less like an order. 'You' before the imperative is rarely used in writing.

Test

Complete these conversations. Put one word in each blank.

1. A: Excuse me. Could you tell me how to _____ to the art gallery?
   B: Certainly. You _____ along this road and _____ the second _____ on the left. Then _____ take the first _____ on the right and the gallery is _____ _____ left.

2. A: Excuse me. _____ you tell me _____ I _____ to Manchester, please?
   B: Yes. You can _____ by bus. That's the cheapest way. Or you can _____ _____ by train or you can fly too.
   A: I see.

3. A: Excuse me. Could _____ tell _____ where the nearest telephone box is?
   B: Sure. _____ along this road to the end. _____ right and _____ the first _____ left and there's a phone box _____ your right.
   A: Thank you very much.

Student B data for information gap exercise on page 32.

FROM LONDON TO	BY BOAT & COACH	BY BOAT & TRAIN	BY PLANE
New York			
Johannesburg	no service	no service	13 hours
Rio de Janeiro	no service	no service	12 hours
Tokyo			
Sydney	no service	no service	29 hours
Paris			
Amsterdam	12 hours	12 hours	1 hour
Stockholm	3 days	28 hours	2½ hours
Rome			
Athens			

5

SUMMARY OF CONTENTS

Functional/notional areas	Describing (1) – Actions
Language item(s)	A. Present Continuous – 'now' B. Present Continuous – Long term developments C. Present Continuous/Present Simple
Topic	The Seaside

Describing Actions

Checkpoint Complete this newspaper article. Choose words from the box below. You may need to put more than one word in each space and use the same word more than once.

am are begin beginning begins come comes coming consider considering considers go goes going improves improves improving increase increases increasing introduce introduces introducing is make makes making need needing needs own owning owns rise rise rises rising rising

LEISUREWEAR LTD, the Manchester company which _____ clothes for many British sportsmen and sportswomen, _____ through a period of great success and good fortune. It _____ even _____ the possibility of moving its head office to London. Robert Houseman, the man who _____ Leisurewear, said yesterday, 'We _____ the quality of our clothes; we _____ new styles, and sales figures _____. Our marketing area _____ and now many European countries _____ to put in orders. We _____ a head office that is in the centre of operations. So London here we _____.'

A Present Continuous – now

1. Listen to the conversation on the tape and answer these questions:

a) Where do you think they are? b) What are they doing? c) What are they holding?

Now look at the eight pictures below and try to put them in the right order. Then listen to the conversation again and check to see if you were right.

2. **Look at the picture. Work in pairs. Say if these sentences are true or false.**

a) Some boys are fighting.
b) A woman is standing on the roof.
c) A girl is sitting on a car.
d) A man is smoking a pipe.
e) A girl is eating an ice-cream.
f) Some men are playing the guitar.

3. Now write down five more sentences about the picture – some true, some false. You and your partner look at each other's sentences. Say which are true and which are false.

4. Work in pairs. Student A look at this page; student B look at the picture on page 45.
There are ten differences between the pictures. Without showing your partner your picture, find out what the differences are.

B Present Continuous – Long term developments

THE CHANGING FACE OF SALCOMBE

SALCOMBE, the Devonshire beach resort, is becoming extremely popular. In the late 1950s there was only one hotel in the town and very few guest houses. Now, however, more and more hotels are starting to open up along the sea front; new guest houses are putting up vacancy signs in the streets near the beach; and young businessmen are moving in and starting up fish and chip shops, restaurants and ice-cream parlours, hoping to make some easy money in the summer months. Life for the locals is gradually losing its traditional sleepy character. They too are beginning to realise the commercial possibilities of tourism. They are changing from a close rural fishing community and becoming a group of sharp business-minded individuals.

1. Work in pairs. After reading the magazine article, decide what you think is happening in Salcombe to:

the beach	the bus company
the cafes	the cinemas
the fishermen	the local businessmen
the shopkeepers	the shops
the taxi drivers	the young people

Example: *The bus company is expanding.*
They are buying more buses.

2. Work in groups. Discuss what is happening to/in:

the world population	the environment
space research	fashion
Central America	the Soviet Union
the world supply of oil	medicine

Add some topics of your own and discuss them too.

3. Work in groups. Discuss what is happening at the moment in:

your life   your town   your province   your country

C Present Continuous/Present Simple

1. Listen to the interviewer and Jack Walters and fill in the table.

NAME	USUAL JOB	SUMMER JOB
Jack Walters		
Elsie Chapple		
Jim Barnes		
Janet Barnes		
Bob Duncan		
Betty Duncan		

ONE interesting change in Salcombe concerns jobs. People who usually _____ one job in the winter now _____ something very different. Jack Walters, who usually _____ behind the bar at the Rose and Crown, and Elsie Chapple, who _____ at the petrol station for most of the year, _____ both _____ ice-creams on the beach. Jim Barnes usually _____ on a local farm throughout the winter but he now _____ a little postcard shop. His wife, Janet, _____ in guests at the moment, whereas she usually _____ at the local supermarket. The Duncans, Bob and Betty, _____ teas in their front garden. But during the winter Bob _____ fishing and Betty _____ at the college in Plymouth. This hard work does have its rewards though. The people of Salcombe can afford Caribbean holidays to get some sunshine in winter!

2. Now complete this article. You may need to use more than one word to fill each space.

3. Roleplay: work in pairs, As and Bs.

Pair A

You are disc jockeys. You usually work for a local radio station on the early morning show. Now you are working at a discotheque in Salcombe for the summer. Think about what you usually do and how your job changes in the summer. Someone is going to interview you. Prepare what you will say.

Pair B

You are going to interview a disc jockey who usually works for a local radio station on the early morning show but is working in a discotheque in Salcombe for the summer. You want to know how different it is. Think what questions you will ask and prepare what you will say.

Now form new pairs (one A, one B) and act out the interview.

4. Who are these people? Where do you think they work? What are they doing at the moment?

Example: He's a cook. He works in a restaurant.
He's reading a book at the moment.

Consolidation

1. Complete this postcard from Gina Walker to her brother, Stephen.

> POST CARD
>
> CORRESPONDENCE   ADDRESS
>
> Steve,
> I'm in Plymouth this week
> for the windsurfing champion-
> ships. I _____ a wonderful
> time. I _____ a lot of
> practice and I _____ learning
> a lot about windsurfing. Also I
> _____ to know lots of
> people that I usually only _____
> at weekends. It's fantastic.
> Hope you are well.
>   Love, Gina
>
> Steve Walker
> 17 Benton Road
> LONDON W18

2. Listen to this interview with Gina. Decide whether the following sentences are true or false.

a) Gina usually goes to Plymouth on Wednesdays.
b) She lives in London.
c) She's a hairdresser.
d) She goes to Plymouth almost every weekend.
e) She stays at a small hotel.
f) She sometimes goes walking.
g) She returns to London on Sunday evening.
h) This week is the Third Plymouth Windsurfing Championships.
i) Gina is having a week's holiday.
j) She's not doing a lot of windsurfing.
k) She's learning a lot about windsurfing.
l) She's having a wonderful time.

3. Read the article about the National Windsurfers Club, then choose the best ending for each sentence.

a) Thousands of young people
   (i) went windsurfing 10 years ago.
   (ii) windsurf nowadays.
   (iii) are joining windsurfing clubs.

b) The NWC are
   (i) starting a school in Plymouth.
   (ii) forming clubs all over the country.
   (iii) very worried.

c) Ken Potter and Linda Gray
   (i) first met last April.
   (ii) meet every six months.
   (iii) are happy about their club now.

d) The NWC organises
   (i) meetings twice a year.
   (ii) championships twice a year.
   (iii) meetings four times a year.

e) Which sentence is false?
   (i) Nobody is interested in the NWC.
   (ii) Windsurfing is more popular than it was 10 years ago.
   (iii) The NWC tried to help windsurfers.

NWC

TEN YEARS AGO there were very few windsurfers in Britain, and no windsurfing organisations. Now, however, thousands of young people go windsurfing every weekend and, more importantly, windsurfing is getting organised. In April last year, Linda Gray and her husband, Kenneth Potter, founded the National Windsurfers Club.

The NWC now advertise in local newspapers all round the country and are trying to start local clubs in as many new towns as possible all round Britain. They are sending representatives to seaside resorts round the country to talk to local windsurfers and find out if they are interested in forming a club. They are also organising championships in four major seaside towns, and at Plymouth, on the south coast, they are starting a special windsurfing school.

Representatives from individual clubs meet every six months at Plymouth to decide how they can help windsurfers round the country. After the last meeting in October Linda Gray said, 'Ken and I were a bit worried at first that nobody would be interested, but now we're really enjoying ourselves. We're getting about twenty phone calls a day from people who want information about the NWC. Windsurfing is becoming really popular!'

4. Work in groups. Imagine that you and the other members of your group are running the local windsurfing club in your town. The club is not doing very well — you are having a lot of problems. Discuss what the problems are, using the present continuous as much as possible. Use the ideas below to help you.

Example: *We aren't getting enough new members.*

membership
subscriptions
meetings
advertising
joining a national organisation

raising money
championships
social activities
etc

Language Summary

Use:

> We use the Present Continuous to talk about actions that are happening now.
> What are you doing?
> I'm listening to the radio.
> He isn't working at the moment.

> We also use the Present Continuous to talk about things which are happening or developing over a longer period of time.
> Venice is slowly sinking into the sea.
> The weather isn't getting any better.
> Is industry in your country expanding?

Form:

I	am	singing.
You We They	are	
He She It	is	

I	'm not	singing.
You We They	aren't	
He She It	isn't	

Am	I	singing?
Are	you we they	
Is	he she it	

Yes,	I	am.
	you we they	are.
	he she it	is.

No,	I	'm not.
	you we they	aren't.
	he she it	isn't.

UNIT 5   45

Test   Fill in the blanks with the correct form of the verb in brackets.

1. A: What's that noise?
   B: Oh! Jack _____ to the radio. (listen)

2. A: What time _____ that shop _____? (close)
   B: Usually at 5.30, but on Thursdays they _____ open late. (stay)

3. A: Is Fred in?
   B: Yes, but you'll have to wait. He _____ his mother. (phone)

4. The sun _____ in the east and _____ down in the west. (rise, go)

5. The population of the world _____ (increase)

6. _____ you _____? I _____ (come, wait)

7. Tortoises _____ for a very long time. (live)

Student B data for information gap exercise on page 39.

6

SUMMARY OF CONTENTS

Functional/notional areas	Past Events Confirming Facts
Language item(s)	A. Past Simple (1) Short Actions B. Past Simple (2) Long Actions C. Past Simple (3) Confirming Facts
Topic	Hospitals

Past Events

Checkpoint   Andrew had an accident yesterday. Look at the pictures and describe what happened.

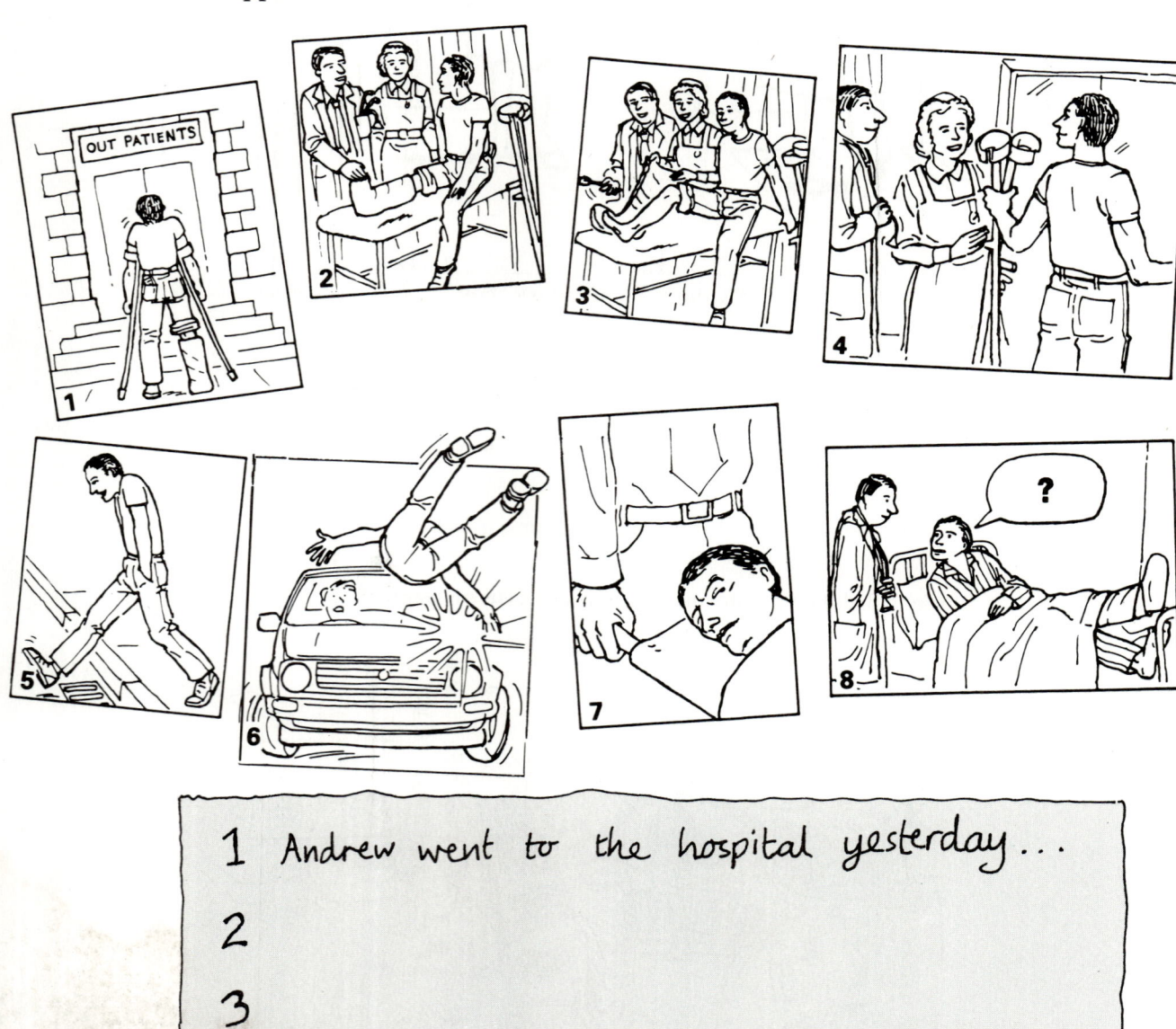

1 Andrew went to the hospital yesterday...

2

3

A Past Simple (1) Short Actions

Grant woke up slowly. His head really hurt. Kirov was a strong man. Looking round, he seemed to be in a hospital. He raised his head a little. It was an ordinary hospital room – a couple of chairs, a table with his case on it, a wardrobe in the corner. There was a half-open door opposite the bed – his own bathroom perhaps. That was nice. He wondered what the time was. His watch was not on the bedside table – probably smashed in the fight.

Carefully he got out of bed and went to the nearest of the two windows. He looked out but the night was dark and he could not see anything. His mouth and his throat were dry so he walked over and pushed the half-open door. It was indeed a bathroom. He drank some water and washed his face, looking at his reflection in the mirror. Suddenly a thought struck him. He rushed back into the room and looked at the other window. My God! There were bars on it. He tore open the wardrobe but it was empty. He ran over to his case and threw it open. It too was empty. He started to run towards the door but it began to open.

'Good evening, Mr Grant,' said Kirov. 'You cannot escape this time.'

1. Draw Grant's movements on the plan of the room like this:

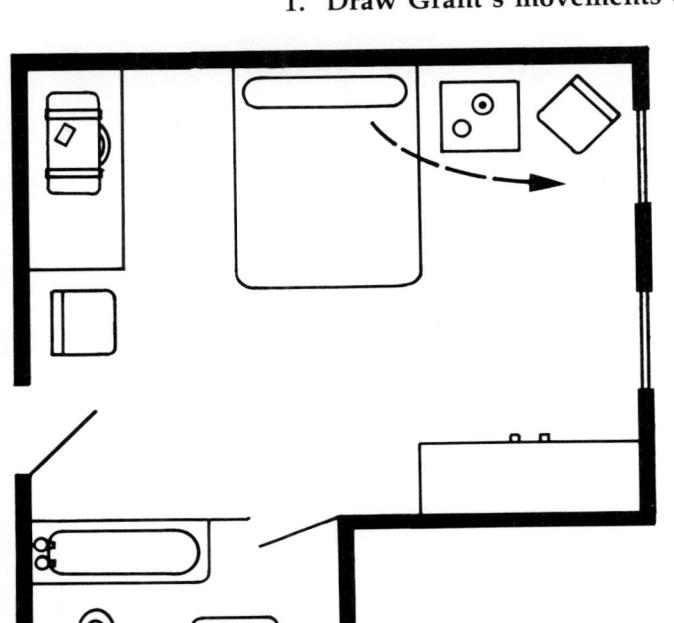

2. Put the words in these sentences into the right order and then decide if each sentence is true or false.

   a) HOSPITAL GRANT AN IN WAS ORDINARY
   b) WARDROBE CASE WAS THE HIS ON
   c) OF HE OUT BED CAREFULLY GOT
   d) OF HE OUT WINDOW LOOKED THE
   e) THE HE DOOR PUSHED BATHROOM
   f) IN HIS WERE THE CLOTHES WARDROBE

3. Find the past tenses of these verbs from the passage:

wake		go		drink		tear	
hurt		look		wash		run	
raise		walk		strike		throw	
get		push		rush		say	

4. Without looking at the passage, try and remember what Grant did. Use the verbs in exercise 3 to help you.

5. Work in pairs. Tell your partner what you did when you woke up this morning. Find out what he/she did.

B Past Simple (2) Long Actions

1. Listen to this interview between a careers advice counsellor and a young unemployed girl. Write down the questions the counsellor asks about the following:

   school:

   subjects:

   sports:

   societies:

   holiday jobs: (1)

   (2)

2. Look at the form that the counsellor filled in for another girl (June Watts). Now fill in the blank form for the girl in the interview in 1 above.

   AVERY CAREERS ADVICE CENTRE

   GENERAL BACKGROUND
   Name: June Watts
   Date of leaving school: 6/87
   Subjects: Good at Maths. Liked English
   Sports: Basketball
   Societies: —
   Job experience: Cleaner for 3 months
   Time unemployed: 12 months

   AVERY CAREERS ADVICE CENTRE

   GENERAL BACKGROUND
   Name: _____
   Date of leaving school: _____
   Subjects: _____
   Sports: _____
   Societies: _____
   Job experience: _____
   Time unemployed: _____

3. Work in pairs. Ask your partner questions and fill in a form for him/her.

4. Work in groups. Ask and tell each other some of the things you did up to the age of fifteen. Talk about:

   - what sports you played (who with, and where)
   - what you did at school
   - what television programmes you liked
   - what you did at weekends/holidays (and where)

UNIT 6   49

C Past Simple (3) Confirming Facts

1. Listen to this conversation in Dr MacGregor's surgery. Who is Dr MacGregor talking to?

2. Listen again to the conversation and complete the two medical report cards below.

```
MEDICAL REPORT CARD
Name: John Michael Smith
Appointment Date: _____
Complaint: _____
Cause: _____
Hospital        ☐ yes   ☐ no
X-ray           ☐ yes   ☐ no
Blood test      ☐ yes   ☑ no
Treatment _____
```

```
MEDICAL REPORT CARD
Name: John Martin Smith
Appointment Date: _____
Complaint: _____
Cause: _____
Hospital
X-ray           ☐ yes   ☐ no
Blood test      ☐ yes   ☐ no
Treatment       ☐ yes   ☐ no
```

3. Listen again and write down the questions the doctor asks about:
   - the appointment: *Didn't we make an appointment for Thursday 14th June?*
   - the bandage: _____
   - hospital: _____
   - how it happened: _____

4. Work in pairs.

   Example: You think your partner went to the same school as you.
   A: *Didn't you go to the same school as me?*
   B: *Yes, that's right/No, I don't think so. I went to ...*

   You think your partner:
   a) had a blue shirt on yesterday.
   b) was in your class last year.
   c) learnt Russian at school.
   d) worked for the Post Office.
   e) was a good footballer at school.
   f) knitted a scarf when he/she was young.
   g) came here yesterday.
   h) was at (your friend)'s party.

5. Write down five things you think your partner did last Saturday. In pairs, try and find out if you are right or wrong.

Consolidation

HEART OP SUCCESS

AT 8.30 yesterday morning seven-year-old Christine Powell walked up the steps of the London Road Hospital, holding her father's hand. She knew that her life was in the hands of Dr Heather Sharp. Surprisingly, she looked very calm. At 10.00 nurses took Christine down to the operating theatre. Dr Sharp spoke to her for about five minutes and explained the operation to her once again. Then the anaesthetist gave her an injection and half an hour later the operation began. Dr Sharp, one of the world's leading heart surgeons, removed Christine's sick heart and replaced it with a man-made one. The operation took five hours. At 4.30 Christine was back in her room sleeping peacefully. Dr Sharp visited her every hour to make sure everything was all right. Christine's parents sat in her room through the night until she woke up this morning cheerful and smiling. She said she didn't feel anything. For seven years she lived with a sick heart; we hope she lives another seventy with her new one.

1. Read the newspaper article 'Heart Op Success', then put these pictures in the right order. Number them 1–6 and write the time for each.

2. Find the words in the article that mean the following:

a) cutting the body to take something out or make it better
b) a special room in a hospital for operations
c) a doctor who gives you something to stop you feeling pain
d) a doctor who performs operations
e) putting liquid into someone with a special needle
f) happy

3. A year later the same newspaper reporter decided to write another article about Christine.
Listen to the conversation he had with Christine's parents before he wrote the second article and make notes below.

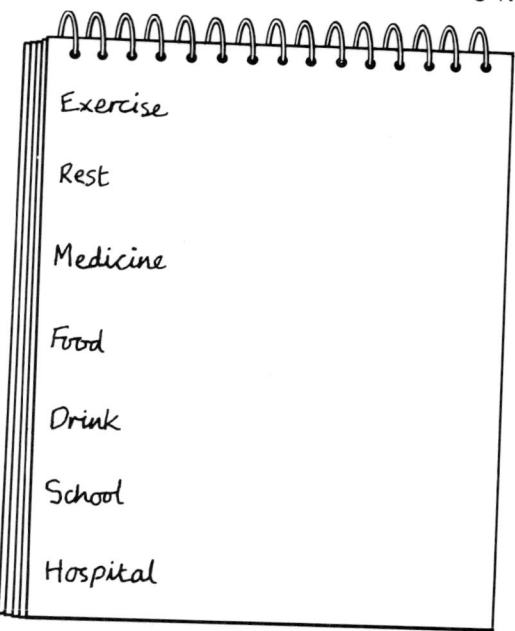

Exercise

Rest

Medicine

Food

Drink

School

Hospital

4. This is the new article that the newspaper reporter wrote.
Complete it by filling in the blanks with the correct past tense of the verbs in the box.

have perform give go cycle take be say sleep go not have cannot want not be have cannot

ON this day last year Dr Heather Sharp, one of the world's leading heart surgeons, *performed* a five-hour operation on seven-year-old Christine Powell, and _____ her a new man-made heart. Today Christine leads the life of a normal healthy child.

At first Christine _____ to rest as much as possible. 'She _____ very tired after the operation,' her parents _____. 'She _____ a lot of the time.' However, she _____ a little exercise. In the mornings she either _____ for a walk or _____ to a nearby wood with her mother. Even when she _____ much better she still _____ a rest every afternoon.

She _____ to take much medicine – only four pills a day. However, she _____ allowed to eat what she _____. She _____ eat cheese or fried foods, and she _____ drink milk.

At first she _____ to the hospital every week for a check-up. But now, she only has to go twice a year. She is back at school, she is full of energy and she seems like any other normal, healthy, eight-year-old – thanks to the wonderful skill of Dr Sharp.

5. Work in groups. Discuss what the newspaper headlines below might mean and what you think about them.

COMPENSATION FOR NEW DRUG DEATHS

Government to spend more money on medical research

Six hospitals to close next year

MORE CUTS FOR HEALTH SERVICE

NURSES TO STRIKE FOR MORE PAY

EMBRYO EXPERIMENT LAW PASSED

Language Summary

Complete the summary by filling in the blanks with the correct form of the verbs in the box.

Use:

> The Past Simple is used to talk about things that happened in the past and are now finished. It can be used for short, quickly finished actions, or for longer actions or situations.
>
> SHORT ACTIONS
>
> I _____ the door.
> Did he _____ that cup?
> You didn't _____ me about that.
>
> LONGER ACTIONS
>
> We _____ there for seven years.
> Did she _____ in hospital for six weeks?
> They didn't _____ there.
>
> The negative interrogative form is often used for confirming facts.
>
> Didn't you speak to the director about it?
> Didn't I say we should meet on Friday?
> Didn't you go to Luxembourg last year?

open	opened
break	broke
tell	told
live	lived
stay	stayed
work	worked

Form:

I You We They He She It	spoke. explained.	I You We They He She It	didn't	speak. explain.

Did	I you we they he she it	speak explain	?

Yes,	I you we they he she it	did.	No,	I you we they he she it	didn't.

Test

Look at the pictures and complete the text below using the verbs on the left.

pass	Last week Gerald _____ an antique shop
see	near his house. He _____ a beautiful
go	painting in the window, so he _____
ask	into the shop and _____ the assistant
be cost	how much it _____. It only _____
buy take	£50 so he _____ it and _____ it home.
come	That evening his sister _____ round to see him.
buy	'Where _____ you _____ that
ask	painting?' she _____.
say	'In the antique shop round the corner,' _____ Gerald.
cost	'How much _____ it _____?' she
ask	_____.
reply	'Fifty pounds. Why?' _____ Gerald.
sell	'Well, I _____ it to them last week,'
say	she _____. 'But I _____ not
get	_____ fifty pounds for it. They only
give	_____ me ten!'
think know	'Oh no! I _____ I _____ that picture!'

7

SUMMARY OF CONTENTS

Functional/notional areas	Past Events
Language item(s)	A. Past Simple and Past Simple Passive B. Past Simple Passive
Topic	News and History

Past Events

Checkpoint What can you say about these?

1. Planted by HRH Duke of Edinburgh 3/6/75
2. Coutts Garage Invoice
3. Mona Lisa
4. Fine English Mustard
5. Marlboro
6. Wimbledon Made in England
7. PASSAGE TO INDIA from the book by E.M. Forster Director: David Lean
8. Made in Japan (binoculars)
9. Made in West Germany (kettle)
10. Italian Vermouth

UNIT 7

A Past Simple and Past Simple Passive

1. Listen to the interview with Prince Kasongo and number the sentences below in the order in which they happened.

- [ ] They tied him up again.
- [ ] They drove him back to London.
- [ ] They treated him well.
- [ ] They put a bag over his head.
- [ ] They tied his hands.
- [ ] They threw him on to the floor of the car.
- [ ] They locked him in the cellar.
- [ ] They drove him out of London.
- [ ] They took him to a house.
- [ ] They pushed him out of the car.
- [ ] They put a bag over his head again.
- [ ] They brought him food and drink.

2. Each of the sentences in 1 above can be changed into the passive like this:

They tied his hands. *His hands were tied.*

Look at the newspaper article below about the kidnapping and complete it using verbs in the passive. Use the sentences above to help you.

KIDNAP VICTIM RELEASED

THIS morning Prince Kasongo, the African prince kidnapped three days ago, was released by his kidnappers. Prince Kasongo's nightmare started on Monday morning when he was attacked by three men. His hands _____ behind his back, a bag _____ over his head, and he _____ on to the floor of the kidnapper's car. Then he _____ out of London and _____ to a house in the country. Once there he _____ in the cellar. According to the Prince himself, he _____ well. Food and drink _____ to him and he was not harmed at all by the kidnappers. Finally, after three days, he _____ again and the bag _____ over his head again. He _____ back to London and _____ out of the car right outside his front door. Strangely, no ransom _____ .

3. Work in pairs. Ask questions to find out information about the people, places and things in Box A. Use the other boxes to help you.

A

America	1989	Alexander Bell	discovered
Julius Caesar	1492	Edmund Hillary	published
Mount Everest	1928	Macmillan	invented
The South Pole	490 BC	Alexander Fleming	assassinated
Penicillin	1889	Christopher Columbus	climbed
The telephone	44 BC	Gustav Eiffel	reached
The Marathon	1953	Brutus and Cassius	built
The Eiffel Tower	1911	Phiddipides	run
This book	1876	Roald Amundsen	

Example: America
A: *When was America discovered?*　　A: *Who discovered it?*
B: *I think it was discovered in 1492.*　　B: *Christopher Columbus.*

B Past Simple Passive

In 1057 the city of Pagan, on the Irrawaddy river, was made the capital of Burma. During the next two centuries many beautiful temples and pagodas were built. These were made of stone. Burmese houses, however, were made of wood. In 1287 the city was destroyed by Kubla Khan. The wooden houses were burnt down but the stone temples and pagodas were not badly damaged. However, the city was never rebuilt. Over the years some temples were destroyed by earthquakes, others by the weather. But even today more than 5 000 pagodas remain – an incredible sight!

1. Read about the city of Pagan, then cover the text and make sentences using the prompts below. Add and change words where necessary.

Example: 1057/Pagan/make/capital
In 1057 Pagan was made the capital of Burma.

a) temples and pagodas/build
b) pagodas/make/stone
c) houses/make/wood
d) 1287/city/destroy/Kubla Khan
e) temples and pagodas/not/damage
f) wooden houses/burn down
g) city/never/rebuild
h) some temples/destroy/earthquakes

2. Make sentences as in the example. Use the words in the boxes to help you.

Example: This coffee was grown in Brazil.

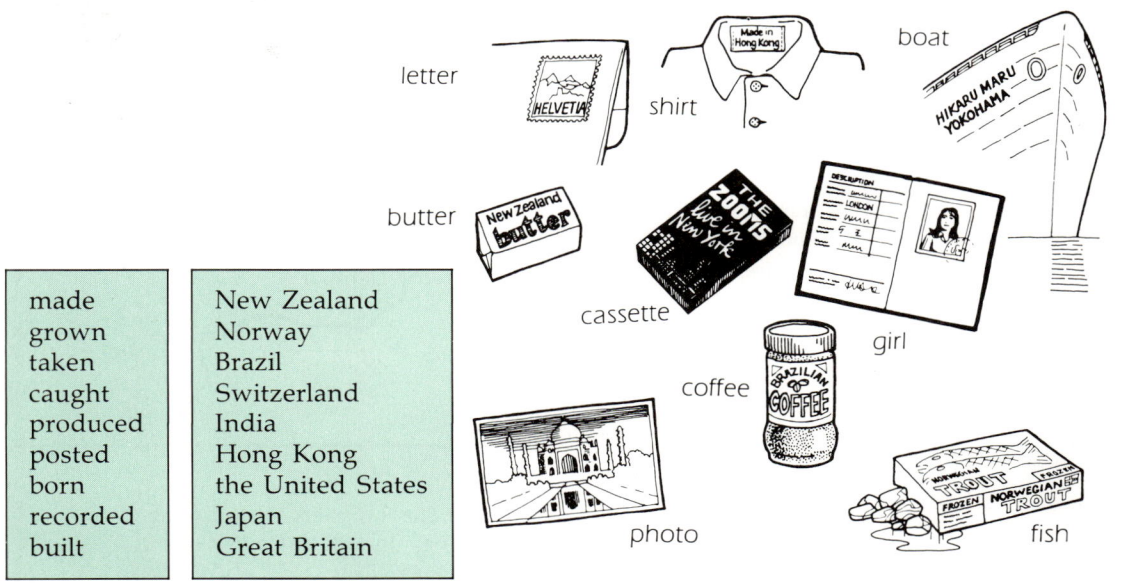

letter shirt boat butter cassette girl coffee photo fish

made	New Zealand
grown	Norway
taken	Brazil
caught	Switzerland
produced	India
posted	Hong Kong
born	the United States
recorded	Japan
built	Great Britain

3. Look at the two pictures of the same garden. The picture on the left shows it in January 1982; the picture on the right in April 1982. What was done to it? Make sentences like this:

The grass was cut

4. Work in groups. Choose something or someone and together think of sentences to describe the thing or person, using the Past Simple passive. Each person in the group writes down the sentences. Then form new groups. Each person in the new group has a different list of sentences, describing a different thing or person. Try to guess who or what each list describes.

Example: He was born in Scotland.
            He was awarded a scholarship to St Mary's Hospital Medical School.
            He was awarded a gold medal by London University.
            Penicillin was discovered as a result of his research.

Consolidation

1. Read the following newspaper article. The sentences are in the wrong order. Number them 1–9 to show the correct order. Then mark the route of the plane on the map.

HIJACKERS CAUGHT

☐ The plane landed in Algiers at about one o'clock local time.

☐ The captain was then ordered to fly to Banjul in The Gambia.

☐ In the early hours of this morning an Ocean Airlines 747 was hijacked on a flight from Nairobi to London via Tunis.

☐ After this the plane was refuelled and took off again.

☐ The plane left Tunis on time at midnight but about 30 minutes later three armed men broke down the cockpit door and ordered the captain to fly to Algiers.

☐ Sometime before dawn they shot their way across the frontier into Senegal where they were captured by the Senegalese police.

☐ The hijackers immediately released all the passengers but the crew were kept on board.

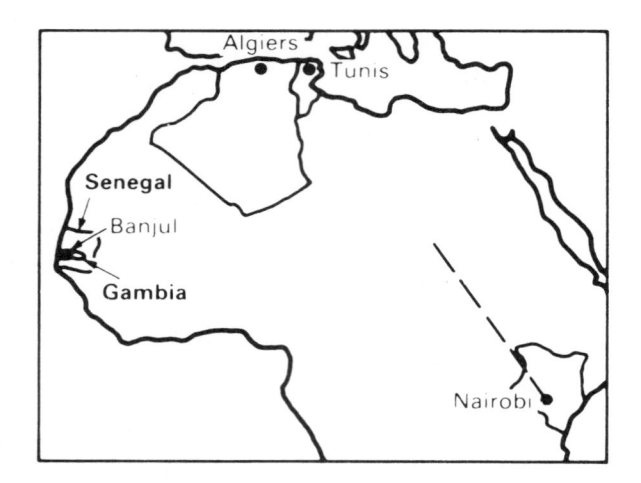

☐ The hijackers tied up the crew, joined their colleagues and escaped.

☐ As the plane landed, it was met by another group of terrorists waiting on the runway with high-speed Land Rovers.

2. Listen to the news broadcast about the hijack. The broadcaster makes five mistakes. Make a note of the mistakes and then write sentences describing them. The first one has been done for you.

The plane was a 747 not a 707.

3. The reporter on the spot heard the news broadcast on the radio and immediately sent a telex to the radio station informing them of the mistakes. Complete the telex with one word in each space.

```
NEWS BROADCAST INCORRECT STOP PLANE 747 NOT
707 STOP PASSENGERS _____ IN ALGIERS NOT
CASABLANCA STOP PLANE _____ TO BANJUL NOT
BISSAU STOP CREW _____ NOT _____ STOP
PLANE NOT _____ UP STOP
```

4. Roleplay: work in pairs.

Pair A
You are the managing director of Ocean Airlines. You are very worried. The newspapers and the radio have different reports of the hijack. Captain Thomas, the pilot of the plane, may be dead. You are going to phone Banjul airport. Prepare what you will say.

Pair B
You are Captain Thomas. You are in a hotel in Banjul, resting after the hijack. The phone rings. It is your managing director. Prepare what you will say.

Now make new pairs (one A, one B) and act out the conversation. Begin like this:

B: Captain Thomas here. Hello?

A: Ah! Captain Thomas. Good to hear you. This is Jack Meads, Managing Director of Ocean Airlines. Can you tell me exactly what happened?

Language Summary

Complete the second part of the summary using words from the box. You will not need to use all the words.

Form:

> They | drove | him | into the country.
>
> *He was driven into the country.*
>
> SUBJECT + TO BE + PAST PARTICIPLE
>
> They | grow | this coffee | in Brazil.
>
> *This coffee is grown in Brazil.*

Use:

> We often use the passive when the subject of the action is unknown or unimportant.
>
> This coffee _____ in Brazil. (I don't know who grew it).
> He _____ up.   (By someone, I don't know who).
>
> We also use the passive to focus attention on what is most important to us and therefore comes first in the sentence.
>
> The car _____ round the corner and _____ down a wall.
> My wall _____ down yesterday.
>
> ---
> grew   grown   tied   swerved   knocked   was   brought

Test   Fill the spaces with the correct form of the verbs in brackets.

1. The police _____ the escaped criminals last night. (catch)
2. Goldfinger _____ by Ian Fleming. (write)
3. In 1966 England _____ the World Cup. (win)
4. Robert Kennedy _____ by Sirhan Sirhan. (assassinate)
5. My fridge _____ last Friday. (not repair)
6. I _____ this dictionary from Kennets Bookshop. (buy)
7. _____ you _____ John last Friday? (see)
8. Michael _____ by train last week. (not come)
9. _____ those photos _____ last year? (take)
10. These songs _____ at last year's song contest. (sing)
11. The children's parents died when they were young, so they _____ by their aunt. (bring up)
12. My bag _____ from my car last week. (steal)
13. When _____ the visitors _____ to arrive? (expect)
14. The painting _____ for a high price. (sell)
15. John's dog _____ the postman yesterday. (bite)

8 SUMMARY OF CONTENTS

Functional/notional areas	Describing (1) – People, Things and Places
Language item(s)	A. Describing People B. Describing Things C. Describing Places
Topic	People, Things and Places

Describing People, Things and Places

Checkpoint   Complete this list by adding the names of other famous people. Say why they are famous. Use *who* or *that*.

Lee Harvey Oswald   *Lee Harvey Oswald was the man*
Leo Tolstoy   _____
_____   _____
_____   _____

What are these things? What do you use them for? Make a single sentence about each one, using *which* or *that*.

a corkscrew   *A corkscrew is a thing*
a screwdriver   _____
a vase   _____
a lawn-mower   _____
a coat-hanger   _____

Complete this list by adding the names of other famous places, and say why they are famous. Use *where*.

Olympia   *Olympia is the place*
Wimbledon   _____
_____   _____
_____   _____
_____   _____

A Describing People

1. Work in pairs. Look at these pictures. Read the nine sentences below and write each man's name and where he lives.

Name _____
Town _____

a) The men who have beards are Mr Fisher and Mr Baker.
b) The men who are bald are Mr Cooper and Mr Cutler.
c) The men that are wearing glasses are Mr Cooper and Mr Barber.
d) The man whose face is scarred is not Mr Fisher.
e) The men that are bald both live in the same place.
f) The men that have glasses both live in London.
g) The man whose tie is striped lives in Aberdeen.
h) The man who has long hair lives in Cardiff.
i) The men that have beards both live in the same place.

Choose the names and towns from these lists:
Names: Fisher, Cooper, Barber, Cutler, Miller, Baker.
Towns: Cardiff, London, Aberdeen.

2. Work in pairs. What happens in your country? Ask and answer questions like this:

Example: A: *What happens to people { who / that } drink and drive in your country?*
B: *They usually lose their licence.*

Ask about people who:
- drop rubbish in the streets
- don't pay their taxes
- don't pay their electricity bill
- travel by train without a ticket
- burgle houses
- cross the street in the wrong place

3. Make sentences. What should these people do?

Example: pets/sick
People whose pets are sick should { ring the vet. / take them to the vet. / go and see a vet.

| teeth/ache | taps/don't work | passports/expired | jobs/boring |
| health/bad | houses/redecorating | cars/broken down | English/not very good |

4. Make sentences.

Example Bob/play tennis/last week
There's Bob. He's the person I played tennis with last week.

a) Angela/have tea/yesterday
b) Dave/borrow £5/last Monday
c) Jill/go to the cinema/next week
d) Jeremy/lend my car/last weekend
e) George and Hilda/telephone/last night
f) Bob and Wendy/have dinner/next Friday
g) Ted and Ginger/see/tomorrow afternoon
h) Elsie and Jane/take to the theatre/tonight

B Describing Things

1. Listen to the tape and fill in the table below.

Name	Designer		Colour	Material
NOEL		Jacket		
		Trousers		
JUSTIN		Jacket		
		Trousers		
SIMON		Sweater		
		Trousers		

What does the announcer say about all the clothes?

2. Now make sentences about all the clothes like this:

The jacket { which / that / ___ } Noel is wearing is made of cotton.

3. Work in pairs. A must close his/her eyes and try to remember what other people in the class are wearing. B must tell A whether or not he/she is right or not.

Example: A: *The trousers that Alphonse has got on are made of leather.*
   B: { *Yes, that's right.*
       No, they're not. They're made of cotton.

4. Look at the picture below for two minutes. Then close your books and try to remember the time on each clock.

Example: *The clock* (that/which is) *behind the door says two o'clock.*

C Describing Places

1. Listen to the conversation between Pete and George and answer these questions.

   a) What happened in Greece? That's where . . .
   b) What happened in Italy?
   c) What happened in France?
   d) What happens in Spain?

2. Work in pairs. Tell your partner either about your experiences in different places, or what you know about them. Ask and answer questions, as in the example.

   Example A: *Have you ever been to San Francisco?*
   B: { *Yes, I have. That's where I met my husband/wife.*
   { *No, but that's where the Golden Gate Bridge is, isn't it?*

   Cairo
   Berlin
   Los Angeles
   Rio de Janeiro
   Singapore

   Sydney
   Tahiti
   Moscow
   London
   Athens

3. Write down the names of five places that have been very important in your life. Work in groups. Tell the other members of your group why these places are important to you.

Consolidation

1. Close your eyes and try to describe the person sitting next to you. The teacher will ask you some questions about him or her too.

2. Divide into As and Bs. As work in pairs and Bs work in pairs.

   A Read Ms Andrea Tipton's statement on page 67 and then do exercise 3.
   B Listen to Mrs Janet Norman's interview with the police and then do exercise 3.

3. Read or listen to the statement from your witness and fill in the Wanted Person's Description Form below.

NORTHSHIRE POLICE
WANTED PERSON'S DESCRIPTION FORM

Name (if known) _____

Height _____

Colour of hair _____

Colour of eyes _____

Build _____

Face _____

Clothes _____

Other features _____

Wanted because of:

Crime _____

Place _____

Date _____

Time _____

signed _____ date _____

4. Now read (As) or listen to (Bs) the statement of your witness. Tick (✓) the adjectives that you would use to describe the witness.

calm ☐ careful ☐ worried ☐ frightened ☐
excited ☐ nervous ☐ observant ☐ upset ☐

5. Now make new pairs (one A and one B in each pair) and compare your descriptions. Work together and decide on the best description of the wanted man. Then copy and fill in another Wanted Person's Description Form for circulation to all the police in the area.

This statement (consisting of .1. page each signed by me) is true to the best of my knowledge and belief and I make it knowing that if it is tendered in evidence I shall be liable to prosecution if I have wilfully stated in it anything which I know to be false or not believe to be true.

signed *Andrea Tipton* dated 22/7/84

On Thursday 22nd July 1984, I went shopping as usual at about 9 o'clock. I probably got to Dalton's Bakers on the High Street at about 9.30. That is where I usually go first. I was in there for about five minutes. As I came out I heard shots. Two men - one of them with a gun in his hand - ran out of Morgan's Bank. A policeman ran out and ordered them to stop. The man that had the gun shot at him but missed and then ran off along South Street. The other robber ran off in a different direction.

I only saw the robber that had the gun. I did not look at the other one at all really. The one who had the gun was about six feet tall with black hair and a beard. His hair was very untidy. He was wearing glasses. He was about medium build and I remember he had a very long nose. The clothes which he had on were a bit dirty. The jacket he was wearing was dirty and torn. It was a black leather one, I think. He had a light blue shirt on that also looked a bit dirty. He was wearing jeans which had a hole in the knee; and he had some brown boots on.

signed *Andrea Tipton*

Language Summary

Complete the summary using the words in the box.

DEFINING RELATIVE CLAUSES

- With people we use _____, _____ or _____.

    The woman _____ has blonde hair is called Jean.

    The boy _____ bicycle I broke was very angry.

- With things we use _____ or _____.

    The pen _____ is on the table doesn't work.

- When _____, _____ or _____ is the object of the relative clause we can leave it out.

    He's the person (that) I had lunch with last week.
    That's the book (that/which) I read for my exams.

- With places we use _____.

    That's _____ I broke my leg.
    London is _____ I was born.

| that | where | which | who | whose |

Test   Complete the sentences with *who, that, whose, which, where,* or *nothing.*

1. Jim's the man _____ I spoke to yesterday.
2. The girl _____ is crying is called Jenny.
3. The man _____ car was stolen is Mr Brown.
4. Where's the boy _____ sells the programmes?
5. Jakarta is _____ I lost my passport.
6. Those are the apples _____ I bought this morning.
7. It's a thing _____ I use for opening bottles.

8. That's the man _____ sister's wedding we went to.
9. Isn't that _____ your flight was delayed?
10. She's the girl _____ saved my life.

9

SUMMARY OF CONTENTS

Functional/notional areas	Comparing
Language item(s)	A. As ... as ... B. Comparatives and Superlatives C. (Not) enough/too
Topic	Transport

Comparing

Checkpoint   Make comparisons about the following groups of items and answer the questions below each group. Use the words in the box at the bottom to help you.

Ford    Rolls Royce    Porsche

Would you like to travel in any of these? Why?/Why not?

biplane    Comet    Concorde

Would you like to travel in any of these? Why?/Why not?

Mount Everest 8848 m    Mont Blanc 4807 m    Ben Nevis 1343 m

Would you like to climb any of these? Why?/Why not?

```
big  comfortable  cheap  dangerous  difficult  enough  expensive  fast
high  long  low  most  short  slow  small  too  useful
```

A As . . . as . . .

1. Read this advertisement. The information on the left has got mixed up. Join the words on the left with the correct information. The first one has been done for you.

Universal Airlines
would like to announce the arrival of their new Jet Class Service

You might like to know about our

- Passengers — ☐ you can come as late as fifteen minutes before departure.
- Seats — ☐ it's as good as in a first-class restaurant.
- Food — ☐ it's not as expensive as you think.
- Check-in — ☐ there aren't as many as on most normal flights.
- Baggage allowance — ☐ they're as big and as comfortable as most airlines have in first class.
- Destinations — ☐ you can have as much as you usually take first class.
- Frequency — ☐ we go to as many as 60 major cities throughout the world.
- Price — ☐ we fly as often as most other major airlines.

For further information ring 01-684-4231 or write to Universal Airlines, Universal House, London W1A 3HP.

2. Work in groups. Look at this table. A marketing company has done a survey of four small airlines.

AIRLINE	CHECK-IN (mins. before departure)	BAGGAGE ALLOWANCE	No. OF DESTINATIONS	FOOD	PRICE RANGE
Universal Airlines	15	30 kgs	60	1st class	C
Oakland Airways	15	20 kgs	60	1st class	B
Juniper Air	30	30 kgs	40	standard	B
Air Brunswick	30	30 kgs	50	standard	A

Price range: A = expensive; B = moderate; C = cheap

Compare the other airlines with Universal Airlines.
Make sentences like these:

The food is not as good on Juniper Air as on Universal Airlines. You can take as much baggage on Juniper Air as you can on Universal.

3. Complete this advertisement for Oakland Airways using *as . . . as . . .*

OAKLAND AIRWAYS
★ You can _____ 15 minutes before departure.
★ You can _____ on a normal flight.
★ You can _____ 60 destinations.
★ The food _____ in a first-class restaurant.
★ You don't pay _____ on some airlines.

B Comparatives and Superlatives

TRAVEL IN THE PHILIPPINES

JEEPNEYS These are the most popular and most typical form of Filipino transport. They are also the cheapest and the most fun for both long and short distances; but not always the most comfortable. Before you leave the Philippines, make sure you have a ride in a jeepney.

TAXIS Taxis are more expensive than jeepneys but still cheaper than in many other countries. In Manila the taxis have meters. In other towns you bargain the price first. Tricycles are usually cheaper.

TRICYCLES These are motorcycles with sidecars. They are cheaper than taxis but still more expensive than jeepneys. It's best to fix the price before you get in.

BUSES For longer distances buses are very economical. They are also more comfortable than jeepneys. If the bus is full, it may leave earlier than scheduled, so get there in plenty of time.

BOATS Travelling by boat in the Philippines is much easier than in other South-East Asian countries. They are cheap, comfortable, and punctual. It does, of course, take longer than flying.

AIRLINES Philippine Airlines (PAL) flies to all the main towns. It is more expensive than the other forms of transport but faster and more comfortable. If you are in a hurry, fly. But don't forget to have one jeepney ride at least.

1. **Read the travel article then compare the following forms of transport in the Philippines. Make sentences as in the example. Use the words in the box.**

Example: jeepneys/taxis

Jeepneys are more fun than taxis.
Jeepneys are cheaper than taxis.
Taxis are more comfortable than jeepneys.

| cheaper |
| more fun |
| more expensive |
| slower |
| faster |
| more comfortable |

tricycles/jeepneys   planes/jeepneys
jeepneys/buses   tricycles/taxis
taxis/buses   planes/buses
boats/planes

2. **What can you say about jeepneys and planes? Make sentences as in the example. Use the words in the box.**

Example: *Jeepneys are the most popular form of transport.*

| the fastest | the most expensive | the cheapest | the most typical |
| the most comfortable | the most popular | | |

3. **Work in groups. Compare different forms of public and private transport in your country. Talk about:**

- planes
- cars
- underground railway
- boats
- taxis
- trishaws
- buses
- bicycles
- coaches
- trains
- helicopters
- motorbikes
- anything else you can think of.

Which form of transport do you prefer to use and why?

C (Not) enough/too

1. Your friend is thinking of buying a new car. There are several points that she thinks are important.

SPEED — it must go faster than 100 m.p.h.
SIZE — it must be big enough for her and her family
COMFORT — it must be comfortable on a long drive
ECONOMY — it must do more than 45 miles to the gallon
PRICE — it must cost less than £6,000

Listen to the conversation in the car showroom. Look at the table and put a tick (✓) if the car is suitable and a cross (✗) if it is not.

CAR	SPEED	SIZE	COMFORT	ECONOMY	PRICE
Nevada					
Dakota					
Indiana					

2. a) What does the woman say about:

- the speed of the Nevada?
- the size of the Nevada?
- the comfort of the Indiana?
- the economy of the Indiana?
- the price of the Indiana?

b) Look at the table and make sentences about the three cars like these:

The Nevada is too small.
The Dakota is fast enough.
The Indiana isn't comfortable enough.

3. Work in groups. Look at the people on the left and the information about the cars on the right. Decide which person you think should have which car.

Granny
Uncle Jack
Jim
Martha
Mum and Dad

Name: Falcon
Top speed (mph) 114
Economy (mpg) 40
No. of seats 4/5
Price £5,750

Name: Kestrel
Top speed (mph) 98
Economy (mpg) 46
No. of seats 4
Price £4,600

Name: Dove
Top speed (mph) 75
Economy (mpg) 62
No. of seats 4
Price £3,150

Name: Hawk
Top speed (mph) 94
Economy (mpg) 51
No. of seats 4
Price £4,200

Name: Eagle
Top speed (mph) 138
Economy (mpg) 31
No. of seats 2
Price £8,900

4. Which of the cars would you like and why? Tell the other people in your group.

Consolidation

1. Read the advertisement for the Business Express and fill in the middle column of the table.

LONDON TO EDINBURGH
THE BUSINESS EXPRESS

Get to Edinburgh with enough time for that important lunchtime appointment. Hold your meetings in the afternoon. Get back as early as 10 p.m.

faster travel for faster people

- ★ stops at Leeds and Durham only
- ★ leaves at 7.30 a.m., arrives at 11 a.m.
- ★ leaves at 6.00 p.m., back at 10 p.m.
- ★ free continental breakfast
- ★ restaurant service on return
- ★ 1st class and 2nd class
- ★ high speed train
- ★ all seats reservable
- ★ from £42 return

Further details at your nearest station.

	BUSINESS EXPRESS	NEW BUSINESS EXPRESS
NUMBER OF STOPS		
TOTAL TRAVEL TIME		
FREE BREAKFAST		
OTHER MEALS		
NUMBER OF CLASSES		
TYPE OF TRAIN		
SEATS		
PRICE		

2. Listen to the conversation about the New Business Express and fill in the right-hand column of the table.

3. Work in pairs. Put the words in the right order to make a sentence and decide if each sentence is true or false. They are all about the New Business Express.

a) earlier it London leaves
b) enough meetings for you time have morning
c) stops has it as before many as
d) before seats more are the than comfortable
e) London back earlier gets it to
f) before faster it's than

4. Work in pairs. Write a new advertisement for the New Business Express. Use some of the language you have learnt in this unit.

NEW BUSINESS EXPRESS

Language Summary

AS ... AS ...

- When two things are nearly equal or similar we can use *as ... as ...*

Flying to New York is *as* expensive *as* going by boat.
I've got *as* many records *as* Bill.
He's almost *as* tall *as* me.

- When we make a negative comparison we can use *not as ... as ...*

It's not *as* cold *as* yesterday.
We haven't got *as* much time *as* we need.

Complete the summary below by filling in the blanks.

COMPARATIVES and SUPERLATIVES

- One-syllable adjectives usually take *-er* and *-est*:

| old | older | oldest |
| cheap | _____ | _____ |

- One-syllable adjectives with one vowel and one consonant double the consonant:

| fat | fatter | fattest |
| big | _____ | _____ |

- Two-syllable adjectives ending in *-y* change *y* to *i* and add *-er* or *-est*:

happy	happier	happiest
lazy	_____	_____
easy	_____	_____

- Other adjectives take *more* and *most*:

interesting	more interesting	most interesting
expensive	_____	_____
common	_____	_____
handsome	_____	_____

- Exceptions:

good	_____	_____
bad	_____	_____
much	_____	_____
little	_____	_____

(NOT) ENOUGH/TOO

- *Enough* comes before nouns but after adjectives and adverbs:

I haven't got enough money.   The doctor didn't come quickly enough.
That's not comfortable enough.

- *Too* is followed by an adjective or an adverb and it can be followed by *for ...* and/or *to ...* as well:

It's too hot.   It's too hot for me.
It's too hot to work.   It's too hot for me to work.

Test Cross out the incorrect form where necessary.

> Well, I wanted to buy the motorbike really. I mean it's *faster/more fast* than the others. But it is the *most dangerous/dangerousest*. Anyway I didn't have *enough money/money enough* so I couldn't get that. I thought about the moped ... it's just as convenient *than/as* the motorbike. In towns it's okay but out in the country it's not as quick *as/than* the motorbike. But the moped was *expensiver/more expensive* than I thought. I was really surprised. It's also really heavy. *Heavier/Too heavy* for me to push up the steps to my house. So I had to look at the bicycle. Of course it was the *most cheap/cheapest*. *Usefuller/More useful* too. I can take it on the train when I go down to see my sister in Bournemouth. She's very old, you know ... even older *as/than* me ... I was the *younger/youngest*. Seven brothers and five sisters I had. Our family was *too big/bigger*, I think. Still, we were *comfortable enough/enough comfortable*. I remember when I was in the army ...

10 SUMMARY OF CONTENTS

Functional/notional areas	Rules
Language item(s)	A. Can/can't/may B. Allowed to/not allowed to/must C. Let/don't let
Topic	Accommodation

Rules

Checkpoint   Complete the sentences using the phrases in the box. Use each phrase once.

> Am I allowed to?   Am I allowed to?
> Can I?   I wasn't allowed to   May I?
> you can't   You must not   You must not
> you're not allowed to   Is it OK to?

Example: *You are coming through customs after your holiday. A customs officer stops you and asks you to open your case. He finds four bottles of whisky. He says, 'I'm very sorry. You're not allowed to bring in four bottles of whisky.'*

1. You've given your best friend a present. You say, 'It's for you, but _____ _____ open it until your birthday.'

2. You are taking an important English exam. You ask the examiner, who you have never met before, 'Excuse me. _____ use a dictionary?'

3. You want to park your car, but a traffic warden comes over to you and says, 'I'm sorry, but _____ park here.'

4. A friend wants you to help her. She says, '_____ borrow your car this evening?'

5. You are in a museum. You are not sure if you can take photos or not. You see an attendant so you ask, 'Excuse me, _____ take photos?'

6. You want to fish in the river but you're not sure about the rules. You ask a passer-by, '_____ fish here?'

7. After two weeks starvation on a health farm, you are talking to your friends. You say, 'It was terrible. _____ eat anything!'

8. You are going to see a friend in hospital and you are walking along the corridor whistling. A nurse comes out and asks you to stop. She says, '_____ make so much noise. The patients are trying to rest.'

A Can/can't/may

1. **Listen to the conversation and answer these questions.**
   - Who is talking?
   - Who is she talking to?
   - Where are they?

2. **Now listen to the conversation again and complete Monica's letter to Cheryl.**

> School Camp (ugh!)
> Windermere
>
> Hi Cheryl!
> Just arrived at camp (yuk! yuk!). It's really boring, of course. This is what we _____ do. We _____ smoke; we _____ drink; and we _____ go to the local pub. But, we _____ go into the local village and, thank heavens, we _____ have tea in the cafe there. We _____ even go fishing. I'd rather eat raw fish than Mrs Jenkins' food - she's a terrible cook! Also we _____ play netball in the field (who wants to play netball in a field?), but we _____ go round screaming and shouting on the camp site. Oh and I nearly forgot, the best part of the whole visit - we _____ stay out until 10 o'clock. BIG DEAL!! I'm longing to get back.
> See you soon,
> Monica

3. **Work in groups. Imagine you are taking a party of fifteen- to sixteen-year-old students on a trip to the places below. What rules would you make for each particular place?**

   - the seaside
   - the capital of your country
   - a farm in the country
   - a sporting event – football match, volleyball match, etc.

B Allowed to/ not allowed to/must

1. Read this notice and fill in the blanks with *allowed to*, *not allowed to* or *must*.

```
         LUCY'S GUEST HOUSE
            HOUSE RULES
```

1. Guests are _____ smoke in the common room but they are _____ smoke in their bedrooms.

2. Guests are _____ keep food in the kitchen, but they are _____ keep any in their bedrooms.

3. Guest are _____ bring alcohol into the house.

4. Guests are _____ play radios, record-players or cassette players, or make a lot of noise between 11 p.m. and 7.30 a.m.

5. Guests are _____ have a shower or a bath between 11 p.m. and 7.30 a.m.

6. Guests are _____ have a maximum of two visistors at any one time.

7. Guests _____ not stick posters or pictures on the walls of their room.

8. Guests _____ not come in later than 12 midnight except by arrangement.

2. Look at the pictures below and decide if what the people are doing is *allowed* or *not allowed* according to the notice above. Who is breaking which rule? Make a list on your own and then compare notes with the person sitting next to you.

3. Work in pairs. Imagine you are about to stay at Lucy's Guest House. You don't know the rules of the house yet. What questions would you ask?

AM I ALLOWED TO SMOKE IN MY ROOM?

4. Work in pairs or groups. What questions might you ask these people in the situations?

- a customs officer when you are going through customs
- a keeper when you are visiting the zoo
- a librarian when you are joining a library
- an attendant when you are visiting an art gallery
- the doctor after you have been to see him/her with a bad cold
- the cashier when you have just opened a bank account
- a nurse when you go to see your friend in hospital

What answers might you get?

C Let/don't let

> Värmlandsgatan 12
> Svedala
> Sweden
> 15th June
>
> Dear Ann,
>
> I'm having a really wonderful time here in Sweden. The family I'm staying with are marvellous. They let me have lots of free time – three afternoons a week and almost any evening I like. They also let me watch their TV, listen to their records, and, best of all drive their car so I can go to Lund or Malmö if I like.
>
> Now here's the bad news! They don't let me come back after 11 o'clock at night and they don't let me cook my own food. Swedish food is okay, but I think it's a bit boring. They also don't let me speak English all the time – but that's quite good. Every morning Mrs Svensson, Karin – her daughter – and I speak Swedish for a couple of hours so now my Swedish is quite good. Skål! Skål!
>
> So I'm really enjoying myself. How about you? And how's life in boring old England?
>
> Write soon. Love,
> Tracy

1. Read Tracy's letter to Ann then make eight true sentences from the table.

The Svenssons let Tracy	stay out late. drive their car. cook her own food. watch their TV.
The Svenssons don't let Tracy	speak English all the time. go out any evening she likes. listen to their records. have three free afternoons a week.

2. Work in groups. Talk about what your parents let/did not let you do when you were children. Tell each other about your childhood experiences. Was it the same with your grandparents? What did they let you do and not let you do?

Consolidation 1. Look at the rules for HMS *Butterfly*. The symbols on the left have been mixed up. Join each symbol to its correct rule. One has been done for you.

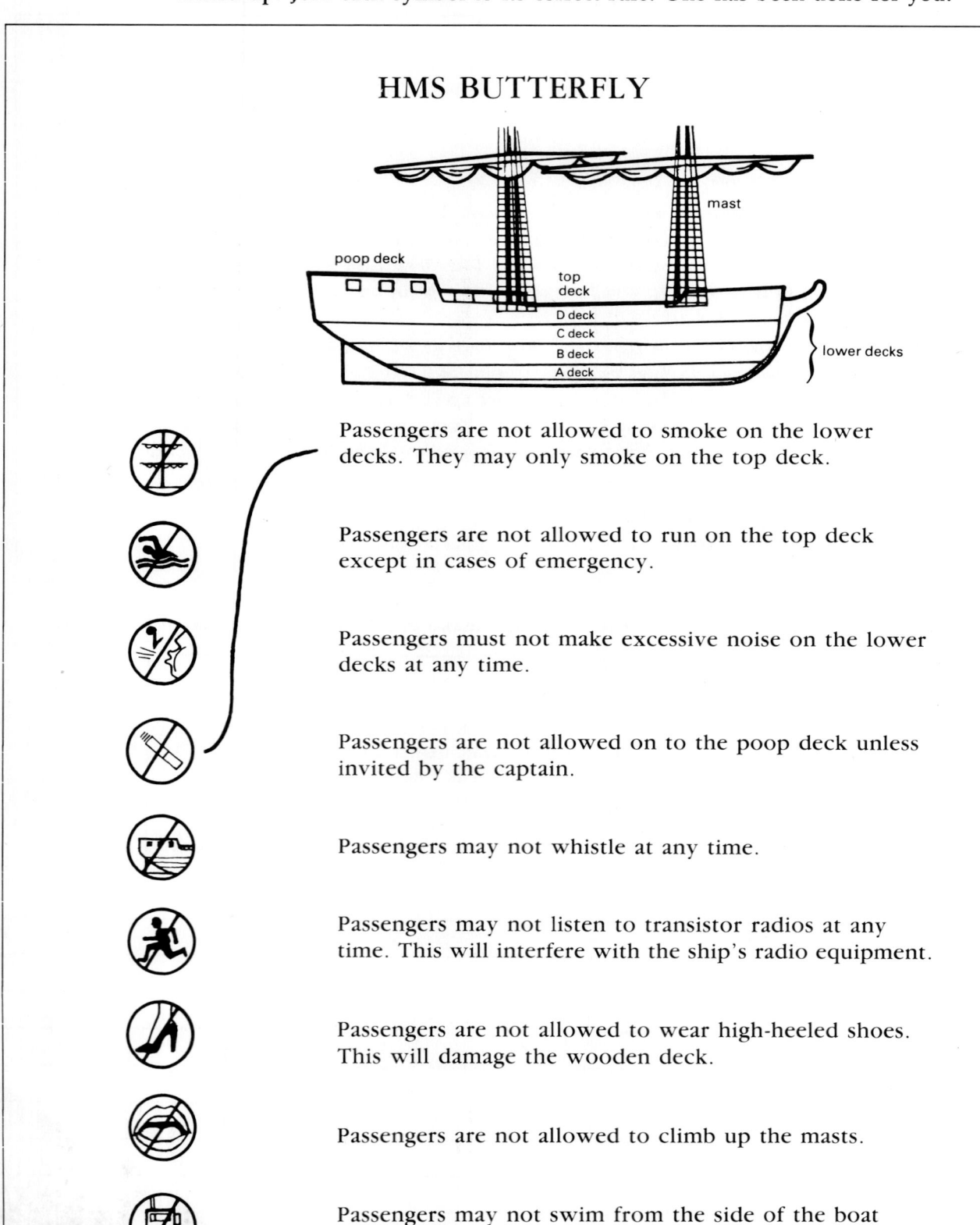

HMS BUTTERFLY

Passengers are not allowed to smoke on the lower decks. They may only smoke on the top deck.

Passengers are not allowed to run on the top deck except in cases of emergency.

Passengers must not make excessive noise on the lower decks at any time.

Passengers are not allowed on to the poop deck unless invited by the captain.

Passengers may not whistle at any time.

Passengers may not listen to transistor radios at any time. This will interfere with the ship's radio equipment.

Passengers are not allowed to wear high-heeled shoes. This will damage the wooden deck.

Passengers are not allowed to climb up the masts.

Passengers may not swim from the side of the boat unless allowed to do so by the captain.

2. HMS *Butterfly* was recently used for an adventure holiday for teenage children. Some of the children did not obey all the rules. Listen to the conversation between the ship's captain and one of the children, Nancy. Look at the symbols again and put a tick (✓) if Nancy broke the rule.

3. This is a postcard from Nancy to her friend, Joanna. Complete the card by unscrambling the sentences in the box and putting them in the right place.

anything do can't	that let either me they didn't do
even can't whistle	them ship the on play we can't
us about let don't run they	I you with camping go may
noise allowed we're not any make to	deck the on can't we go poop

Dear Joanna,
I'm having a horrible time. There are lots of awful rules. The captain's taken away my trumpet because <u>we're not allowed to make any noise</u>, and he's also got my radio because _____.
I _____ because the sailors don't like it.
_____ on the deck and _____ which is the most interesting part of the ship. That's where the captain lives. When I tried to climb the mast to get a good view _____.
We _____.
_____ next year instead?
love,
Nancy

Joanna Beckwith,
The Grange,
Poynton,
Amersham,
Bucks.

4. Roleplay: divide into As and Bs. As work in pairs and Bs work in pairs.

A
You are the manager of the Dragonfly seaside holiday camp for fifteen- to eighteen-year-olds. You are going to tell a new employee about the rules of the camp. Decide what rules you will make and prepare what you will say to the new employee.

B
You are a new employee at the Dragonfly seaside holiday camp for fifteen- to eighteen-year-olds. You are going to meet the manager to find out about the rules of the camp. Decide what questions you will want to ask and prepare what you will say.

Now make new pairs (one A and one B in each pair) and act out the conversation.

Language Summary

Complete the following summary with the correct form of words and phrases from the box.

be allowed to   can   may   must   may   be allowed to   may   can   be allowed to

RULES/RESTRICTIONS

Informal   You _____ use my pen.

You can't smoke in here.

_____ we go to the village?

_____ we have a party?

You _____ come back when you like.

You _____ not fish here.

Am I allowed to take photographs?

You _____ (not) play radios.

You _____ have visitors.

Formal   You _____ (not) take photos here.

We can also use *let* when talking about rules and restrictions, often when referring to the past.

They let us stay out late.
She didn't let me watch television.
Did your parents let you drink wine?

Test

Are the following appropriate or inappropriate? If inappropriate, suggest a better way of saying the same thing.

1. You see someone smoking in a no-smoking area. You say, 'I'm sorry but you're not allowed to smoke in here.'

2. You are at a friend's house. You want to have some more coffee. You ask, 'Am I allowed to have some more coffee?'

3. You are in your bank manager's office. You want to have a cigarette. You ask, 'May I smoke?'

4. You want to see your niece who's just had an operation in hospital. You ask the nurse, 'Am I allowed to see my niece yet?'

5. Your plane stops for an hour in Frankfurt on its way from London to Dubai. The stewardesses allow you to stay on the plane. You tell your friend later, 'They let me stay on the plane.'

6. Your boss wants to change your job without consulting the union. This is illegal. You say, 'You can't do that.'

7. The customs officer notices you have 500 cigarettes as you enter the country. He says, 'You can't bring 500 cigarettes into the country.'

8. The council has stopped people fishing in the local river. You say to a friend, 'They don't let us fish there any more.'

11

SUMMARY OF CONTENTS

Functional/notional areas	Permission
Language item(s)	A. Permission – Informal/Neutral B. Permission – Formal C. Refusing Permission
Topic	Jobs

Permission

Checkpoint   Fill in the blanks in the spaces below. Use the words in boxes (1) and (2) to help you.

- ___(1)___ if ___(2)___ ?
- ___(1)___ mind if ___(2)___ ?
- Is there ___(1)___ ___(2)___ ?
- Would it ___(1)___ ___(2)___ ?
- With ___(1)___ ___(2)___ .

(1) mind would you
    any objection
    your permission
    be possible
    would you

(2) I opened the door?
    I make a cup of coffee?
    I should like to leave?
    to have an ashtray?
    to giving Mr Jones promotion?

What would you say in these situations?

1. You are talking to a close friend. You want to borrow her tennis racquet.

2. You are talking to your uncle. He is old, rich, and he doesn't like you very much. You want to use the swimming pool at his house.

3. You are talking to your sister/brother. She/He wants to wear your best dress/suit.

4. A close friend borrowed a book from you last week. He asks if he can keep it for a few more days. You tell him he can.

5. You are a new member of the board of directors of your company and you are at your first board meeting. The other directors are all very formal. You are rather nervous. You want to leave because you have a plane to catch.

6. You are talking to an acquaintance. She wants to borrow your car tomorrow. Unfortunately you have to go to Bristol.

Now look back at each of your answers. Are you asking for permission, giving permission, or refusing permission?

A Permission – Informal/Neutral

1. Listen to the conversation and answer these questions.

What do Mark and Phil do?
Where is Phil going?
Where is Mark going?

2. Listen to the conversation again and write down the words Phil uses when asking permission concerning the following things:

the Hasselblad   _Would_
the Porsche   _I wonder_
the film   _Okay_
the tripod   _Mind_
the telelens   _All right_
the hotel   _Would_

Now listen again to the conversation and write down the words Mark uses when giving or refusing permission about the same things.

3. You are staying with a friend before going for an important job interview. You are not very well prepared. Look at the list below; what will you ask your friend?

Example: Your pen has run out. *Mind if I borrow your pen?*

You need some paper.
You don't have a briefcase.
You forgot your toothbrush.
Your socks/stockings have a big hole in them.
It's raining and your umbrella is broken.

Your suit/dress is dirty.
You don't have a belt.
You forgot your comb.
You need a car to get to the interview.
You forgot to go to the bank yesterday.

What answers do you think you will get?

4. Roleplay: Divide into As and Bs. As work in pairs and Bs work in pairs.

Pair A
You are about to leave the house before taking an important exam. You are also very late. List eight problems that you have. You are going to ask your brother/sister for help. Practise what you will say.

Example
1 no pen
2 no watch
3 broken ruler
4 bike has a puncture

Pair B
Your brother/sister is always disorganised! He/she is taking an important exam and is late. Can you help with his/her problems? Look at 1–4 in A. Are you going to give or refuse permission when you are asked?

Now make new pairs (one A and one B in each pair) and act out the conversation.

B Permission – Formal

```
OFFICE MEMO                                    Date: 11/7/
From: D. Black
To:   L. Harvey

With your permission I should like to make a change in the
personnel of our department.

I should like to promote Mr Slater to the post of Senior Marketing
Representative, where his overseas experience will be most useful.
Then I should like to advertise his present position. Do you have
any objection to this arrangement?

Might I also have your permission to attend the Senior Executive
Sales Conference in Blackpool from 14th - 18th September?
```

1. Read the first office memo. Underline or write down the phrases Mr Black uses to request permission from his boss.

```
OFFICE MEMO                                    Date: 12/7/
From: L. Harvey
To:   D. Black

I can see no objection to the promotion of Mr Slater and it seems
perfectly acceptable to advertise his post.

I am sorry but I can only allow you to attend the Blackpool
Conference from 14th - 16th September. I see that none of the
talks on the 17th and 18th are of special interest to our company.
In view of this and the economy measures, I'm afraid I can only
allow you to go for two days this year.
```

2. Read the second memo. Underline the phrases Mr Harvey uses to give or refuse permission.

3. Roleplay: divide into As and Bs.
As work in pairs and Bs work in pairs.

Pair A

You have just become the Principal of the school you are now attending. Make a list of the changes you would like to make and prepare for a meeting with the owner. Think about the size of classes, the facilities, the food, student welfare and accommodation, the fees, etc.

Pair B

You are the owner of the school you are now attending. You are about to have a meeting with the new Principal who may want to make some changes. Think about what changes he/she might want to make. Think about the size of classes, the facilities, the food, student welfare and accommodation, the fees, etc. Prepare for the meeting. Decide what sort of things you will not allow. You don't want to lose too much of your profit.

Now make new pairs (one A and one B in each pair) and act out the meeting.

C Refusing Permission

1. Which answer goes with which note? Write the correct names at the top and the bottom.

> Dave,
> Do you mind if I borrow your car next Friday? I'm going down to London.
> Marion

> Jackie,
> Is it okay if I borrow your blue dress for the disco on Friday?
> Pam

> Ms Janet Brown,
> Would it be possible to come and see you at 3.00 p.m. on Friday?
> John Bakewell

> Sorry. I spilt coffee on it last weekend and it's got to go to the cleaner's.

> I'm sorry but I'm afraid I've got meetings all day Friday. How about Monday morning?

> Sorry. I'm afraid I need it. I've got to go to Sheffield.

2. Now fill in the blanks in these notes and write notes in reply refusing permission.

> Silvia,
> ___ I borrow your suitcase next weekend? I'm going to Rome.
> Maurice

> Mr Barnett,
> ___ it be ___ for me to finish your report next week instead of this?
> Mrs Appleby

> Les,
> Mind ___ I take your copy of Wittgenstein to do some revision this weekend?
> Colin

3. You have an important English exam on Saturday morning. You decide to plan your final week's revision before the exam. Look at the plan below. You decide to do three half-days revising your notes (N), three half-days revising grammar (G) and two half-days working in the language laboratory (L). Plan your week and write G, L or N in the plan below.

Monday	
Tuesday	
Wednesday	
Thursday	
Friday	
Saturday	

You should now have two free periods left. Because you missed some lessons, you need to borrow someone else's grammar workbook for one period and someone else's notes for one period. Go round the class asking people if they can lend you their notes (N) or workbook (G) for those free periods. If they can, write it on your plan; if not, ask someone else. You cannot change your plan and you cannot study in the evenings because you are working in a restaurant.

Consolidation Graham Hunt is in charge of the motor pool at Winlock Ltd. When he comes in to work on Monday there are always some notes waiting for him and some messages on the ansaphone.

1. Listen to the messages on the ansaphone and complete the table.

NAME	CAR(S)	DAY REQUIRED
Arthur		
Lady Rosemary Winlock		
Jack Bonham		
Julia		
Molly Saunders		

2. Now read these messages in preparation for (4) below.

Mr Hunt
Would it be possible to have a Porsche for Thursday and Friday?
Sue Bowler

Graham,
Do you think I could have the Astra one day next week?
Cheers
Brian

Mr Hunt,
Could I have a car on Wednesday, please?
Roy Hill

Graham,
Okay if I have something on Friday? Don't mind what.
Christine

Mr Hunt,
Do you have any objection to showing me what vehicles we have in the motor pool? I'll come round on Saturday morning at about 10 o'clock.
Sir Reginald

3. There is a list of seniority at Winlock Ltd. If two people want the same car, the highest person on the list gets it. Here is the list.

Sir Reginald Winlock	Christine Martin
Lady Rosemary Winlock	Arthur Brittain
Molly Saunders	Roy Hill
Jack Bonham	Brian Teacher
Sue Bowler	

4. Work in pairs. Look at the information from the ansaphone in (1) above and the messages (2). Plan who will use the cars on each day of next week. Don't forget to look at the list of seniority in (3) as well!

Monday:	Porsche: BMW: Astra:
Tuesday:	Porsche: BMW: Astra:
Wednesday:	Porsche: BMW: Astra:
Thursday:	Porsche: BMW: Astra:
Friday:	Porsche: BMW: Astra:
Saturday & Sunday	CLOSED

5. Write notes to the people who either cannot have cars or who need more information.

Language Summary

REQUESTS FOR PERMISSION

Fill in the spaces below with the expressions from box (1). Put the expressions in order of formality with the least formal at the top and the most formal at the bottom.

Informal ↑

Okay if I borrow your pen?
All right if I make a cup of coffee?

Do you mind if I smoke?

Do you have any objection to going abroad?
Is there any objection to opening a new shop?

↓ Formal

(1) With your permission I should like to leave.
Mind if I open the window? Can I borrow your pen?
Would it be possible to change jobs? Could I see your passport?
I wonder if I could borrow your toothpaste?
Would you mind if I looked in your bag?

GIVING PERMISSION   REFUSING PERMISSION

Fill the spaces below with expressions from boxes (2) and (3). Put the expressions in order of formality, with the least formal at the top and the most formal at the bottom.

Informal ↑

Go ahead.

Yes, that's all right.
No, not at all.

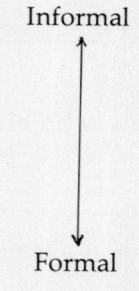

I'd like to but ...

I'm sorry, I'm afraid ...

↓ Formal

(2) Of course. Fine.
That seems perfectly acceptable.
I can't see any objection.
Sure.

(3) I'm afraid ...
'Fraid not.
I'm very sorry, I'm afraid ...
I'm very sorry, but that's not possible.
Sorry.

REFUSING PERMISSION

If you refuse permission in English, you almost always give a reason. It is impolite not to. Often the reason is some other obligation.
Sorry, I've got to drive to Dublin tomorrow.
I'm very sorry, but I'm using it myself.

Test

Complete the blanks in the dialogues below.

1. A: _____ if I sit down?
   B: No _____.
2. A: I _____ if I _____ borrow your car.
   B: _____ that's _____.
3. A: _____ I see your driving licence?
   B: Of _____.
4. A: Do _____ objection to coming on Friday instead?
   B: I'm _____ but I've _____ to go to Dover on Friday.

Say whether the following utterances are acceptable or unacceptable.

1. (a) A good friend is staying at your house. He wants to make a cup of coffee. He says, 'Okay if I make a cup of coffee?'
   (b) You reply, 'That seems perfectly acceptable.'
2. You are in the boss's office asking him for a day's holiday.
   You say, 'All right if I have Friday off?'
3. (a) Your neighbour asks if he can borrow your lawnmower. He says, 'I wonder if I could borrow your lawnmower.'
   (b) You reply, 'I'm sorry, I'm afraid you can't.'

4. You are a very junior member of the board of directors of a company. It is only your second board meeting. You say, 'With your permission I should like to make a suggestion.'
5. Two friends: (a) 'Okay if I take a sheet of paper?'
               (b) 'Sure. Go ahead.'
6. A business colleague has invited you to dinner at his house. You have known him for some years but have never been to his house. You ask, 'Might I have your permission to smoke?'

12

SUMMARY OF CONTENTS

Functional/notional areas	Decisions for the Future Thinking about the Future
Language item(s)	A. Going to B. Verb + to C. Verb/adjective + (that) + clause
Topic	Holidays

The Future

Checkpoint Talk about the pictures below using as many of the phrases in the box as you can.

. . . going to . . .	. . . intending to . . .	. . . hope (that) . . .
. . . hoping to . . .	. . . expect (that) . . .	. . . decided to . . .
. . . decided (that) . . .	. . . planning to . . .	. . . expecting to . . .
. . . sure (that) . . .		. . . should think (that) . . .

A Going to

1. Listen to the conversation and answer these two questions:

What's Bob going to do this year?
What's Maria going to do this year?

2. Listen to the conversation again and mark Bob's route on the map below. Then decide if these sentences are true or false.

a) Bob's going to hire a car in Athens.
b) He's going to visit Delphi to see the temple.
c) He's going to see the Olympic Games.
d) He's going to see the ancient city at Sparta.
e) He's going to visit Argos.
f) He's going to see a play at Mycenae.
g) He's going to see a play at Epidavros.
h) He's going to visit the Parthenon.

3. Look at the contents of Maria's suitcase in the picture. What's she going to do on holiday this year? Make sentences.

Example: *She's going to fly to Rio.*

4. Work in groups if possible. Talk or write about what you have decided to do:

- this week
- next month
- this year
- on holiday this year

B Verb + to

> Salisbury
> 17 March
>
> Dear Martha,
>
> I just thought I'd write and tell you what the family were all planning to do this summer. Norman and I have decided to go to China for three weeks! I'm really excited. We've got all the brochures and we're busy finding out the best way to go. Tim has bought an old Volkswagen camper and he's planning to drive round Europe in it with a couple of schoolfriends. He's hoping to be back in time to go to university in October. Muriel is expecting to find out the results of her exam soon. I think I told you she's hoping to get a job as a research assistant. If she gets it, she won't have to start until September so I think she's intending to go up to Edinburgh for a week or so.
>
> So we're going to have a really busy summer. What about you? What are your plans? Drop us a line soon.
>
> Love,
> Pat

1. Read Pat's letter and make seven true sentences.

Pat and Norman	have	intending		have a busy summer.
Tim	is	going		go to China.
		decided	to	get a job as a research assistant.
Muriel	are	expecting		drive round Europe.
		planning		go to Edinburgh.
Pat and her family	has	hoping		be back by October.
				find out her results.

2. Work in pairs if possible. Imagine a friend of yours is coming to visit you for a couple of days in the town you are in now. Decide what you will do for those two days. Think about these ideas and others:

- museums
- theatre
- discos
- cinemas
- zoo
- restaurant

When you have finished, either tell the rest of the class about your plans, or write them down.

C Verb/adjective + (that) + clause

1. Listen to the conversation between the marketing manager of Transglobe Holidays and his assistant, Mr Philpott, and complete the notes below.

```
LONG HAUL HOLIDAYS
Advertising in _____ papers
              _____ windows
              TV
              Local _____ _____
              nothing _____
Long haul: necessary sales increase _____ %
Short haul: necessary sales increase _____ %
Report ready in        hours
```

2. Now complete the marketing manager's report to the directors using the words in the box.

Report to Directors: Advertising campaign proposal 85/6

With your approval I have decided that our new advertising campaign this year _____ on the long haul holiday sector. If we advertise as usual, I fully expect that we _____ a larger number of enquiries about long haul packages and I therefore hope that we _____ a greater volume. To pay for a campaign advertising short haul holidays an increase in sales of 33% is necessary. The figures of my assistant, Mr Philpott, shows that he is sure an increase of only 18% in sales _____ for this campaign.

I am sure that you _____ his report carefully, and I hope that our proposal _____ with your approval.

J.M.W. Brice

| will receive |
| will study |
| will concentrate |
| will sell |
| will pay |
| will meet |

3. Think about your country/the country you are in now. What can you predict about its future? Make brief notes, giving reasons, on the following. Use the phrases you have learnt so far in this unit.

- unemployment
- the standard of living
- the population
- the health service
- the climate
- the school system
- taxes
- the economy

Consolidation

1. Listen to the advertisement on the radio and make notes below about the jobs that are advertised.

```
JOBS - UNIVERSAL HOLIDAYS
Languages: _____
No. of jobs: _____
Time spent abroad: _____
Time spent at home: _____
Length of training course: _____
Salary: _____
Phone no: _____
Ask for: _____
Write to: _____
```

2. Now read the information sent by Universal Holidays.

UNIVERSAL HOLIDAYS
Ref: UH/LR/361-6

Post: Travel Courier

Universal Holidays, one of the country's leading tour operators, is planning to employ five new travel couriers. We expect that successful candidates will have a good academic record, a smart appearance, and speak one foreign language fluently. We also expect that they will be friendly, communicate well and be efficient and courteous in dealing with the problems that occur in the course of their work. We are especially hoping to receive applications from young language graduates.

While working in Britain, couriers will help co-ordinate our overseas operations and also help organise our U.K. tours. Abroad, couriers will be expected to take full responsibility for the organisation and welfare of tour groups coming out from England.

We are intending to pay a salary of £9,500 for the first year, including the six week training course.

Please return completed application form to the Personnel Manager, Universal Holidays, Universal House, London W1A 3HP.

Find the words in the passage that mean:

a) people who want to be chosen for a job
b) working well and without waste
c) polite
d) to happen
e) somewhere foreign (1)
f) somewhere foreign (2)
g) having the duty of looking after something
h) comfort and happiness

3. Now look at the job application form and complete it.

UNIVERSAL HOLIDAYS

Application for the post of _____

Application reference no. _____

FULL NAME (underline surname) _____

ADDRESS _____
_____

Age _____   Marital Status _____

ACADEMIC RECORD (from the age of 16)

Dates	School/University/College	Exams taken	Grades

EMPLOYMENT RECORD

Dates	Employer	Position

WHY DO YOU WISH TO WORK FOR UNIVERSAL HOLIDAYS?

REFEREES

1.	2.

Signature _____
Date _____

FOR OFFICE USE
Int   Y☐ N☐
Acc   Y☐ N☐
Rej   Y☐ N☐
*1715061

Language Summary

> We use *going to* when we talk about something happening in the future that has already been decided or that is intended.
>
> Are you going to bring the children?
> He isn't going to come.
> She's going to look for a new job.

Fill the gaps in the summary with the correct expression from the box.

> to express intention
> to predict what might happen

> When we are thinking about the future we use the verbs below
> + *to* + *infinitive* – generally _____
>
> We're intending to go by car.
> Are you hoping to see Janet?
> They're planning to join us later.
> She's expecting to receive it today.
> What have you decided to do?
>
> ---
>
> We use the verbs below
> + *that* + a clause – generally _____
>
> I expect (that) I'll see you later.
> We hope (that) you'll be able to come.
> He's decided (that) they'll leave early.
> I shouldn't think (that) we'll be late.
>
> NB: Also *adjective* + *(that)* + *clause*
> Are you *sure* (that) he'll arrive on time?

Test

Fill the blanks with appropriate statements about the future.

1. Jim's exam is on Friday. He's been revising every night for the last two months. He's _____

2. Harry said he'd be here at six o'clock but the traffic's always terrible at this time of day. I _____
3. We _____ to have a party on the sixteenth.
   We _____ you can come.
4. Look at those black clouds. It's _____
5. Why are you carrying your tennis racquet? Are you _____
6. That programme's very late. It doesn't start till 12.30.
   I _____
7. What _____ next Saturday?
8. We _____ to fly to Barbados this summer.
9. Are you _____ anywhere nice for your holiday this year? No, we can't afford it. We're _____ camping instead.
10. Eric has put his name down for football practice on Saturdays. He's _____ be selected for the college team next season.
11. When do you _____ to hear whether you've got the job?
12. Susan hasn't _____ what she wants _____ when she leaves school.

13

SUMMARY OF CONTENTS

Functional/notional areas	Talking about Sensations and Appearances
Language item(s)	A. Can B. Like/as if (though) C. Seem (to)
Topic	Illness

Sensations and Appearances

Checkpoint   Secret Service Agent 006 has fallen into the hands of an unfriendly power. He has been put inside a soundproof steel box with no light, suspended weightless in water for 36 hours. What problems do you think he has? There are at least five!

Describe how the people in these pictures look/feel/seem.

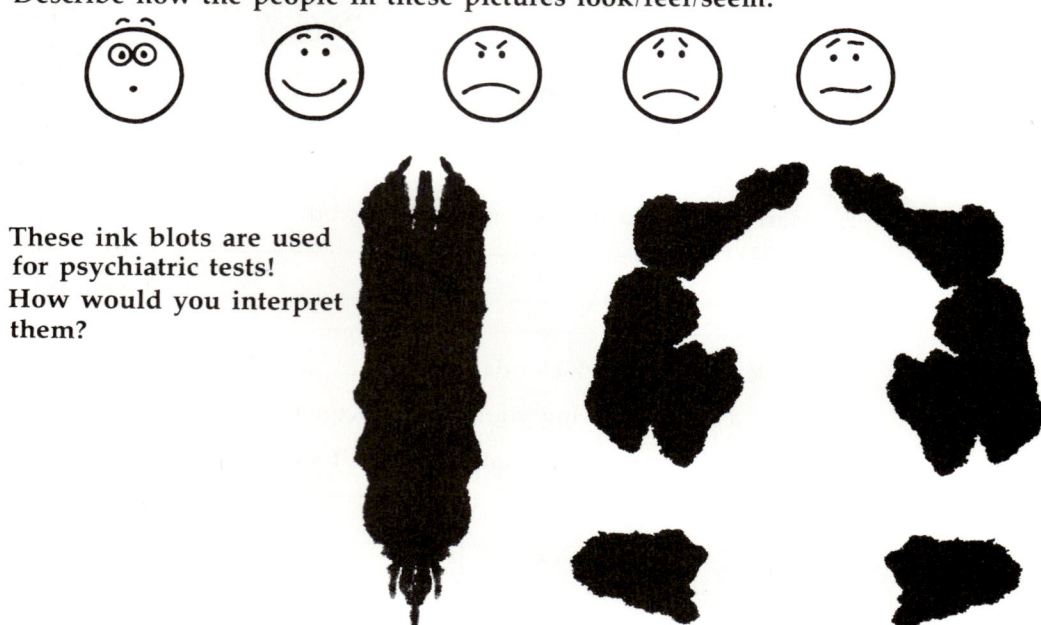

These ink blots are used for psychiatric tests! How would you interpret them?

What can you say about these pictures? How do the people look? How do you think they feel? What do you think is happening?

A Can

1. What does Simon say about:

- the sea breeze?
- the roar of the waves?
- the fishing boats?
- the harbour?
- fresh fish?

> Whiteley Convalescent Home
> Whiteley-on-Sea
> Yorkshire
> 17th Nov
>
> Dear Sylvia,
>
> Thanks for your 'Get Well' card. This 'holiday' of mine is really working. I feel so much better already.
>
> I often go down and walk along the seafront here. It's really marvellous. You can feel the sea breeze blowing through your hair; you can hear the roar of the waves crashing onto the sand; and you can see the brightly-painted fishing boats going out of the harbour in the morning and coming back in the evening.
>
> I sometimes walk all the way down to the harbour itself and watch the fishermen. You can smell the fish a long time before you actually get to the harbour. There are some superb restaurants there. Fish is, of course, the speciality and it's always absolutely fresh. You can really taste the difference!
>
> Well, thanks again for the card. The doctors here say I should be back home fairly soon and then back to work soon after that. So I'll hope to see you before the New Year perhaps.
>
> Best Wishes,
> Simon

2. Complete the questions in this questionnaire using each of these verbs: *smell, see, taste, feel, hear*. Then make up an extra question (b) for each.

QUESTIONNAIRE

1. (a) _____ you _____ the difference between margarine and butter?
   (b) _____

2. (a) _____ you _____ the difference between a compact disc recording and an ordinary cassette recording?
   (b) _____

3. (a) _____ you _____ the difference between a cotton and a polyester shirt when you're wearing it?
   (b) _____

4. (a) _____ you _____ the difference between cheap perfume and expensive perfume?
   (b) _____

5. (a) _____ you _____ the difference between a Renoir and a Manet?
   (b) _____

3. Work in pairs. Ask your partner the ten questions in your questionnaire. Write down the answers.

B Like/as if (though)

1. Listen to the conversation between Ethel and Freda in the doctor's waiting room and fill in the table below.

ETHEL	THE MAN
feels _____	looks like _____
feels as if _____	looks as though _____
	his face looks _____
MRS CHALMERS	FRANK
looks _____	feels _____
looks as if _____	looks _____
looks like _____	seems _____

2. You have just enrolled at the Laurence Richardson School of Acting, where the emphasis is on how you feel, what you feel like doing, and becoming the character you are acting.
Work in pairs. Take it in turns to be the drama teacher and the student, using the following photographs as prompts as in the example below.

Teacher   Okay. You've seen the photo. You're that tramp. Tell me how you feel!
Student   Hungry. I feel hungry. I feel wet, cold and hungry. And not just hungry. Angry! I feel angry too. I feel angry with society.
Teacher   What do you feel like doing?
Student   I feel violent. I feel like stealing something. Why do they have everything while I have nothing? Oh . . . but now I feel tired . . . I feel very tired . . .

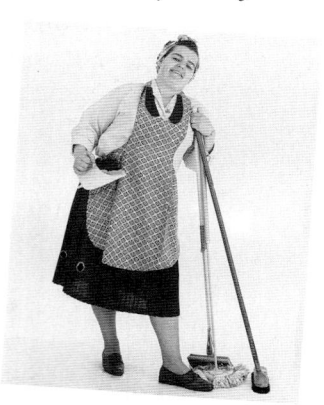

3. Work in groups. Talk about these pictures. What do you think has happened? How do you think the people concerned feel? When you have finished, tell the rest of the class what conclusions you reached.

C Seem (to)

1. Listen to the conversation between Mr Marriott and the doctor. The sentences below all come in the conversation. Number them in the order which they occur.

They seem all right too.
You seem to have lost a bit of weight.
That seems to be okay.
I seem to be terribly tired.
You don't seem to have any problems there.
I'm not surprised you seem to feel tired.
You seem to have been extremely healthy in the past.
It seems to be a strange sort of hobby.

2. Look at pictures 1 to 3 and make sentences as in the example.

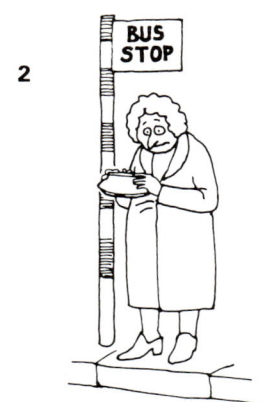

He seems to have been shopping.
He seems to have lost his keys.

3. Roleplay: divide into As and Bs. As work in pairs and Bs work in pairs.

Pair A

You are a doctor. You are about to examine a patient. This patient often comes to see you but there usually isn't anything wrong. Follow the procedure below:
1. Greet the patient and ask what is wrong.
2. Take pulse: it is apparently normal.
3. Feel forehead: no fever or high temperature.
4. Look closely at eyes: apparently normal.
5. Ask patient to breathe in and out: apparently normal.
6. Tap knee gently: apparently normal reactions.
7. Tell patient he/she has a bad case of hypochondria (imagining one is ill).

Decide together what you will say to the patient during the consultation and while you examine him/her.

Now make new pairs (one A and one B in each pair) and act out the conversation.

Pair B

You are the patient. The doctor is about to examine you. She/he never believes that there is anything wrong with you. You don't trust her/him.
1. Tell the doctor you often feel tired.
2. Tell her/him you think you have a fever/high temperature.
3. Tell him/her your eyes get tired and you sometimes have double vision.
4. Tell her/him you get out of breath very easily.
5. Tell her/him your reactions are slow and you always feel very tired.
6. When she/he tells you what is wrong ask her/him for some pills to cure it.

Consolidation

1. Listen to the conversation between the hospital administrator and the nursing sister and make notes in the table below about the patients in St George's Ward at the London Road Hospital.

NAME	DAY SISTER'S REPORT	NIGHT SISTER'S REPORT
Ann Marples		
Eliza Jones		
Carol Newman		
Sue King		
Maria Orsini		
Jackie Lyons		

2. Now read the memo that Mrs Williams left for the Sister to read and make notes about the two new patients.

LONDON ROAD HOSPITAL

Memorandum

From: Mrs Williams

To: Sister - St George's Ward

These are the two new patients arriving today

Nina Porter : She is extremely ill and it looks as though she will be in hospital for some time. She must have as much rest and quiet as possible and must not be disturbed. She needs a lot of sleep.

Clare Quinn : She is coming in for an operation on her leg. We are hoping that she'll only need to stay a couple of weeks. She's usually very friendly and cheerful but her doctor says that she doesn't feel very happy about having the operation.

NAME	NOTES
Nina Porter	
Clare Quinn	

3. Work in pairs. Use the notes you have made in exercises (1) and (2). Look at the plan of St George's Ward and decide how you would rearrange the patients to make them all happier.

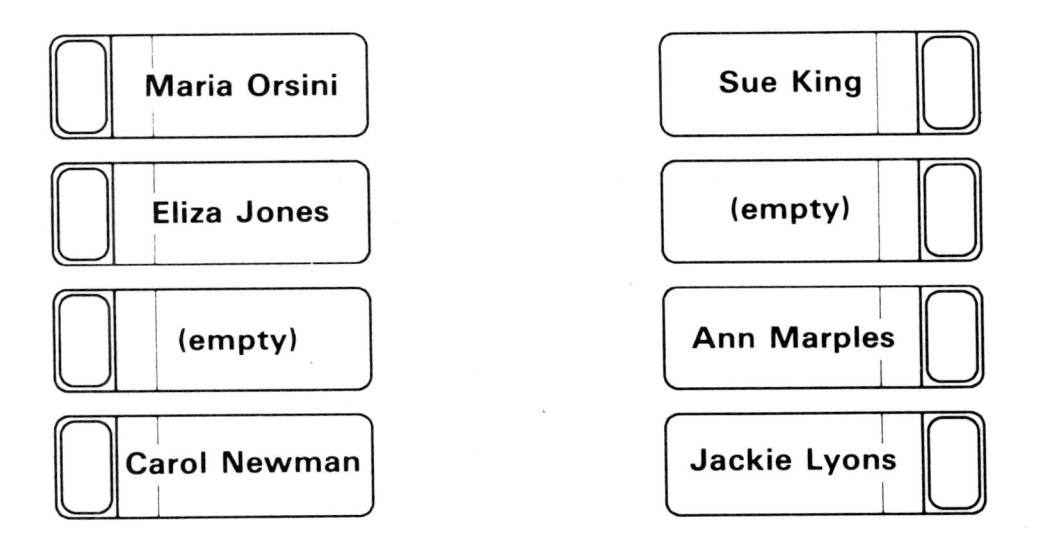

Maria Orsini	Sue King
Eliza Jones	(empty)
(empty)	Ann Marples
Carol Newman	Jackie Lyons

4. Now write a memo from the Sister to the hospital administrator saying what you have done and whether it seems to be successful.

MEMORANDUM

Language Summary

Fill in the blanks in the summaries below using words from the appropriate boxes. You may need to use the same word more than once.

CAN

Instead of using continuous tenses with verbs of the senses (*see, hear, feel, taste, smell*) we usually use *can + the infinitive* (omitting *to*).

I can _____ smoke.
I can't _____ John.
Can you _____ the spices?
I can _____ something on the back of my neck.
Can you _____ the music?

| feel |
| hear |
| see |
| smell |
| taste |

LIKE/AS THOUGH (IF)

With nouns (and gerunds) we use _____.
He looks _____ a tramp.
I feel _____ an idiot.
I feel _____ having a bath.
It sounds _____ a nightingale.

With verbs we use _____ or _____.
It seems _____ he's going to be late.
Does she look _____ she's passed her exams?
I feel _____ I'm going to be sick.

With adjectives we use _____.
She seems _____ intelligent.
Doesn't he look _____ ill?
I feel _____ really happy.

| nothing |
| like |
| as if |
| as though |

SEEM

With *seem* we can also use *to + infinitive*.
He seems to understand it.   They seem to have left early.
She seems (to be) hard-working.
NB *to be* can be omitted when used with an adjective – look at the third example above.

Test

1. What would you say in the following situations? Complete the sentences.

a) Your nose tells you that the oven is on fire. You say, '_____ you _____ something burning? I think it's the oven!'

b) You are lost in the countryside in a fog, but there is possibly a light shining in a house in the distance. You say, 'I think I _____ _____ a light over there.'

c) Your neighbour is playing his radio too loudly. You say, 'Would you mind turning that down? We _____ _____ ourselves speak!'

d) You have broken your leg and the doctor has given you a pain-killing injection. He asks you if you are comfortable. You say, 'Yes. It's okay now. I _____ _____ anything.'

e) You are having a meal at a very expensive restaurant with your friends, but you have a terrible cold. You say to one of your friends, 'I expect the food is really good but I _____ _____ anything!'

2. Complete this conversation. Sharon is visiting her boyfriend, Jason, in hospital. Put *feel, look, (not) seem (to), as if, as though*, in the blanks.

Sharon: What's the matter, Jason? You _____ really bored.
Jason: I _____ really bored. I hate hospitals. And I hate hospital food. Every time the food comes round I _____ I'm going to be sick. And it _____ I'm going to be here for another month at least. Oh! Look out! Here comes Sister O'Hooligan.
Sister: Ah, Jason! And how are we today? Come on, sit up straight. I've brought you your medicine!
Jason: Oh no! Not that! It's horrible.
Sister O'Hooligan holds his nose, lifts his head and pours the green medicine down his throat.
Sister: Good boy! Well done!
Jason: Groooooh!
Sister: Ah! You must be Jason's girlfriend. This medicine _____ be doing him very much good, I'm afraid. Still he _____ mind it!
Jason: Grooh! I feel sick.
Sister: Nonsense! You can't _____ sick. You've just had your medicine.
Jason: I know. That's why I _____ sick.
Sister: Nonsense. You _____ understand. The medicine will make you _____ better.

14 SUMMARY OF CONTENTS

Functional/notional areas	Obligation
Language item(s)	A. Must/have to B. Mustn't/don't have to
Topic	Foreign Travel

Obligation

Checkpoint Complete the following dialogue using *must, mustn't, have to,* or *don't have to.*

Anne: Jack! You _____ forget to go to the dentist's this afternoon.
Jack: No, I know. I _____ remember to take my cheque book too. I didn't pay him last time.
Anne: Are you going anywhere else while you're in town?
Jack: Yes, I _____ to the post-office to collect a parcel or something. The managing director asked me to fetch it for him. Apparently it's very urgent – something to do with an order from America.
Anne: Oh! Right. Now, what about our holiday tickets? Will they be ready yet?
Jack: No, I don't think so. We _____ collect them until a couple of days before we go.
Anne: But we _____ pay for them before then, don't we?
Jack: No, no. We left a deposit. That's enough.
Anne: Oh good! By the way I _____ have a look at my passport and check that it's valid. I might _____ get a new one. That usually takes a couple of weeks, doesn't it?
Jack: Something like that, yeah! Right. Well, I'm off then.
Anne: Okay. 'Bye, darling. By the way, you won't _____ go to the garage – I filled up with petrol yesterday.
Jack: Mm. Thanks. I _____ leave you the car more often – save myself a bit of money. See you.
Anne: 'Bye.

A Must/have to

1. Listen to the conversation between Lesley Upton and Eric Wardle, the joint managers of International Marketing plc, and complete the table below.

NAME	DESTINATION	DEPARTURE DATE	MESSAGE
CASTLE			
BURTON			
McDONALD			
FRAZER			
O'MALLEY			
EVANS			

2. After the meeting Lesley wrote messages to all the reps. Look at the first message and then complete the others. Remember the difference between *must* and *have to*.

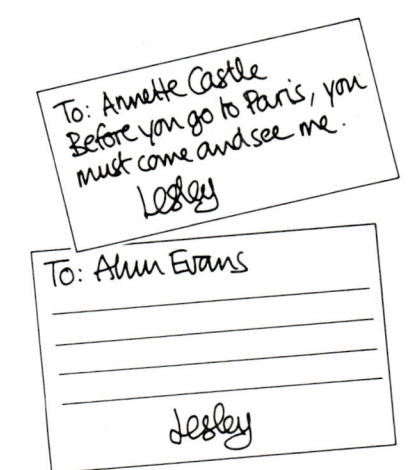

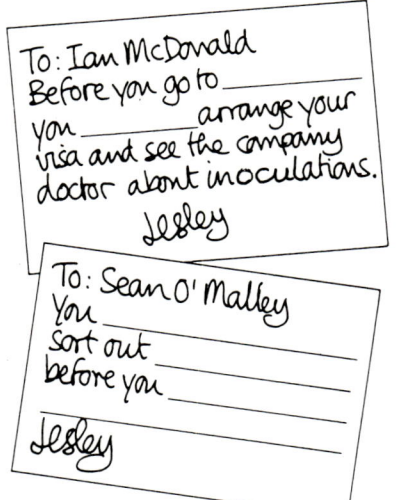

> To: Annette Castle
> Before you go to Paris, you must come and see me.
> Lesley

> To: Ian McDonald
> Before you go to _____ you _____ arrange your visa and see the company doctor about inoculations.
> Lesley

> To: Ray Burton
> When you get back from Nairobi, you _____ go to St Pancras Hospital.
> Lesley

> To: Alun Evans
> _____
> Lesley

> To: Sean O'Malley
> You _____ sort out _____ before you _____
> Lesley

> To: Eileen Frazer
> Before _____ don't forget you _____ get your visa. Also, you _____ come and collect some new samples.
> Lesley

3. Make suitable responses as in the examples.

- The boss wants to see me.   *I have to see the boss.*
- My bicycle has a puncture.   *I must mend it.*
- My French colleagues can't speak English.
- I've got an awful cold.
- I want to stop smoking.
- I've got terrible toothache.
- I need a visa to go to Libya.
- The doctor told me to take more exercise.
- The taxman wants me to fill in this form.
- My company is sending me to Wales.
- Conway sounds a beautiful town.
- I'm really thirsty.

4. Work in groups. Tell each other about the things that you *must do* and the things that you *have to do* during the next month or so. If you need more help, look at the language summary at the end of this unit.

B Mustn't/don't have to

> 36 Denmark Rd,
> Birmingham B1 6GQ
>
> Dear Paul,
>
> Thanks for your letter. Lucky you – going to India! I had a really marvellous time there last year, and I'll certainly give you some tips.
>
> Obviously you have to have a passport, but as you're British you don't have to get a visa. If you want to stay longer than 90 days you can always get a visa while you're there. Also, you don't have to get a health certificate. However, if you're going on to any other countries after India, it might be a good idea to get one. You can't get any Indian currency before you go, and remember you mustn't bring any out with you when you leave. It's against the law and you can't use it anywhere else anyway!
>
> Health of course is the major worry. In theory you don't have to have any inoculations at all before you go, but go and see your doctor and ask him about it. I had injections against polio, typhoid, tetanus and cholera. Remember to take some anti-malaria tablets too. When you're there, don't forget – you <u>mustn't</u> drink the water, and you <u>mustn't</u> eat uncooked food. These are really important.
>
> If you come up to Birmingham sometime, let me know. We can go out for a drink and I'll tell you some good places to go to.
>
> All the best,
> Barry

1. Read Barry's letter to Paul then complete the table. Put a tick (✓) in the appropriate column.

		TRUE	FALSE
a)	Paul doesn't have to take a passport.		
b)	He doesn't have to get a cholera inoculation.		
c)	He mustn't have any inoculations.		
d)	He mustn't eat salad.		
e)	He mustn't bring Indian currency back to England.		
f)	He doesn't have to see his doctor.		
g)	He doesn't have to take anti-malaria tablets.		
h)	He mustn't eat cooked food.		

2. Work in pairs.
You and your friend are going on holiday to Uganda. Look at the items below. Check with each other about what you *don't have* to do and what you *mustn't forget* to do.

Example: A: *We mustn't forget the air tickets.*
B: *Right — but we don't have to take our raincoats.*

3. Work in groups. Discuss what tourists who come to your country *mustn't* do and what they *don't have* to do. Make a list.

4. Before you left for Uganda, you wrote this note to a friend who is going to stay in your flat while you're away. Complete the note with *don't have to* or *mustn't*.

Dear Bella,
Have to rush or I'll be late at the airport. There are a few things I forgot to tell you. I watered the plants before I left so you _____ water them until Saturday. You _____ worry about feeding the cat either. I knew you'd forget so I took her to my mother's!

If the landlord rings, you _____ tell him you're living there. He'd go mad. Just say you're visiting and I'm out. And if he comes round, he _____ see the bathroom. I broke the mirror in there last week and I know he'll throw me out of the flat if he finds out about it. Don't worry about Oscar. You _____ give him any food. He won't want any until I get back. Most goldfish die of overfeeding. If you move his bowl, you _____ leave it in the sun — unless you want fish for supper.

love, Joyce

Consolidation 1. Read about Ubiquity Travel then put these words in the right order to make sentences and mark them true or false.

UBIQUITY TRAVEL

You tell us where to go—
we provide a vehicle and a guide

Guidelines for Africa

PASSPORTS —You have to have a valid passport for all African countries. Make sure it's valid till the end of the trip. Make sure you have plenty of empty pages—some immigration officers like using their stamp.

VISAS —You must get your own visas before the start of the trip. You will have to have a visa for most African countries—find out from their embassies.

IVC —You must get an international vaccination card before departure. You will probably have to have cholera and yellow fever inoculations. You don't have to have any others, but we recommend immunisation against typhoid, tetanus, polio and tuberculosis.

MEDICAL INSURANCE —You must arrange your own medical insurance before departure.

IDL —One other person in the group must have an international driving licence. Other members do not have to have them, but it is helpful.

☐ a) PASSPORT NEED NEW NOT A YOU DO
☐ b) AFRICAN ALL A VISA COUNTRIES NEED FOR YOU
☐ c) MOST YOU HAVE HAVE FEVER COUNTRIES YELLOW AFRICAN TO A INOCULATION FOR
☐ d) INOCULATION YOU POLIO HAVE A MUST
☐ e) MEDICAL MUST INSURANCE YOU ARRANGE
☐ f) LICENCE AN EVERYONE DRIVING MUST INTERNATIONAL HAVE

2. Listen to the interview between Sheila Parfitt and Brian and make notes on what Sheila says about:

- health
- clothes
- bargaining
- accommodation

3. Work in groups. Look at the map of Africa. Your group is doing a trip with Ubiquity Travel. Plan your trip – decide where you want to go, what you will take with you, where you will stay, etc.

4. One member of your party was absent when you were deciding about the trip. Write them a letter telling them what you have decided, what they must bring, what visas they have to get and so on.

Language Summary

Complete the summaries by filling the blanks with *must, have to, mustn't,* or *don't have to* as appropriate.

MUST or HAVE TO
When the obligation comes from the speaker we use _____

    You _____ be back at 6 o'clock.
    I _____ buy a new watch.

When the obligation comes from someone else we use _____

    I _____ be there to meet the new staff.
    I _____ wear a dark suit.

MUSTN'T or DON'T HAVE TO
When there is an obligation NOT to do something we use _____

    You _____ smoke.
    They _____ leave the room.

When there is NO obligation we use _____

    We _____ get up early tomorrow.
    We _____ get a visa.

Test Complete the following sentences using *must, mustn't, have to,* or *don't have to.*

1. I've got terrible toothache. I _____ see the dentist.
2. It's all right. I've found my pencil so I _____ use yours.
3. He insists. I _____ be there at 7 o'clock.
4. Please remind me. I _____ leave my umbrella behind.
5. It says on the invitation. We _____ wear fancy dress.
6. I _____ ring Jane and check that she's coming to collect us.
7. Ssshhh! You _____ make a noise.
8. You _____ to go to the bank. I can lend you some money.
9. Tourists _____ have a visa to visit the United States now.
10. My new job pays more money, so I _____ work overtime any longer.
11. I _____ write to my brother and tell him the news.
12. We _____ move out of our flat by the end of June.
13. You _____ look so worried – I'm not angry!
14. My cousin _____ take her dog to the vet because it's ill.
15. Transport will be provided, so you _____ take your car.

15

SUMMARY OF CONTENTS

Functional/notional areas	Advice
Language item(s)	A. Should/ought to B. Informal Advice C. Formal Advice
Topic	Personal Problems

Advice

Checkpoint Fill in the blanks in the speech bubbles.

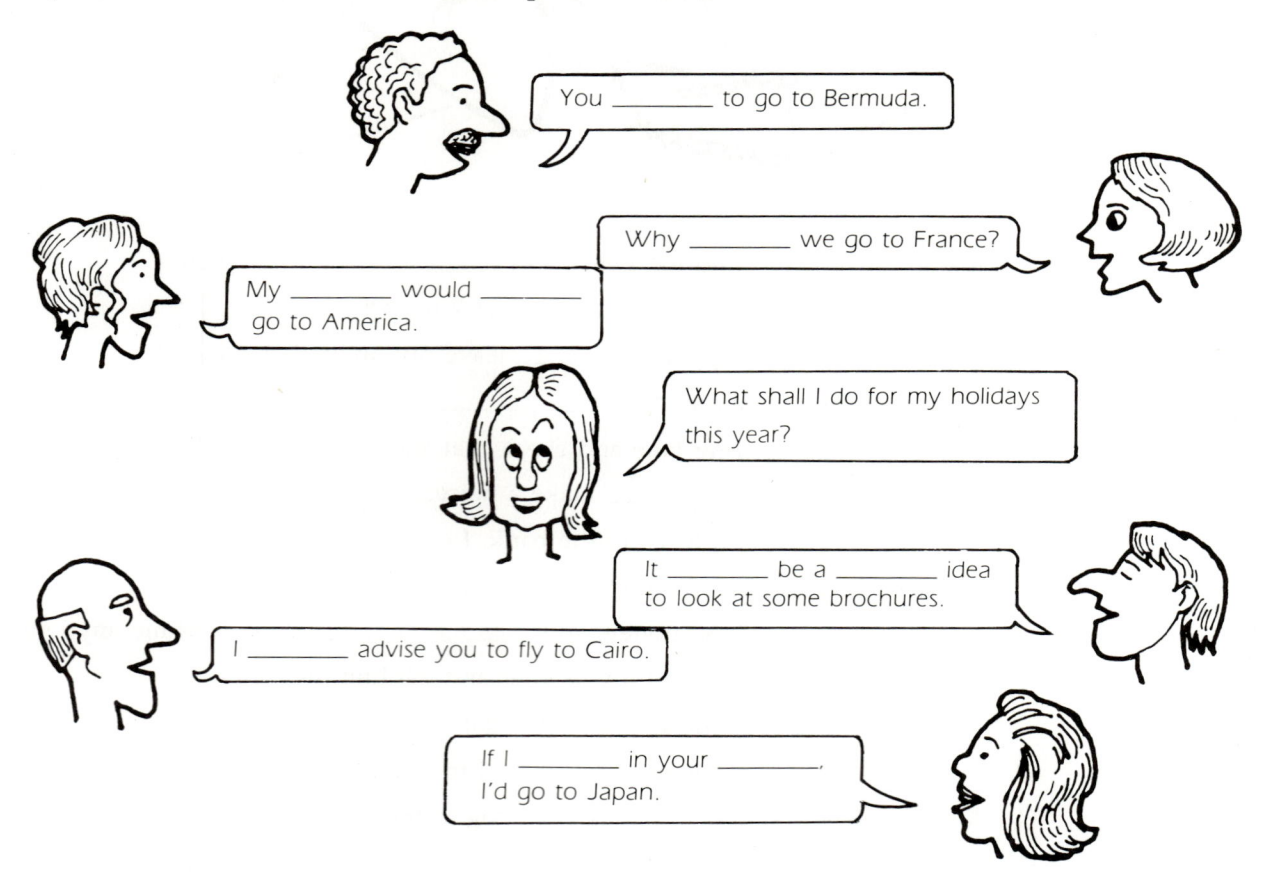

You _____ to go to Bermuda.

Why _____ we go to France?

My _____ would _____ go to America.

What shall I do for my holidays this year?

It _____ be a _____ idea to look at some brochures.

I _____ advise you to fly to Cairo.

If I _____ in your _____, I'd go to Japan.

What advice would you give in these situations?

1. Your friend doesn't know where to buy a new kettle. He asks your advice.
2. A senior business colleague, who you don't know very well, is flying out to Africa. She doesn't know which inoculations to get. She asks your advice.
3. Someone stops you in the street and asks you if you can tell them where there is a good restaurant.
4. A close friend can't decide which school to go to to learn English. She asks your advice.

A Should/ought to

1. Match the pictures on the left with the words on the right.

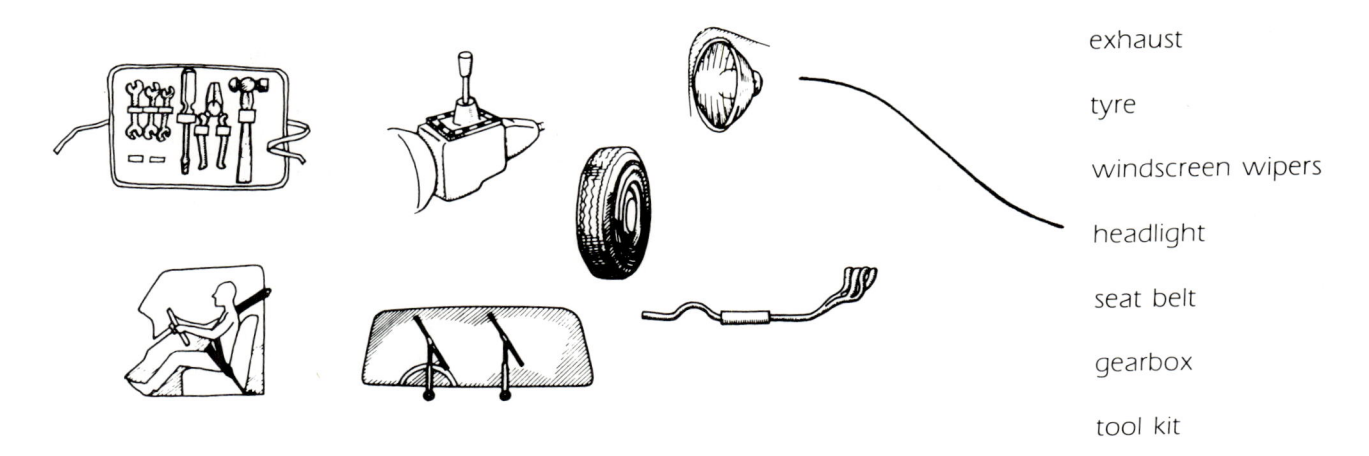

exhaust

tyre

windscreen wipers

headlight

seat belt

gearbox

tool kit

2. Now listen to the conversation between Roger and his father and fill in the table.

PART OF CAR	FAULT	FATHER'S ADVICE
exhaust		
tyres		
windscreen wipers		
headlight		
seat belts		
gearbox		

3. Work in groups. Student A look at this page; the rest of the group look at page 125.

A: You are going for a job interview and you want some advice from your friends. Decide what sort of job you are applying for, where it is and exactly where you hope to work (what department, etc). Fill in the following notes so that you can tell your friends a little about the job.

NOTES

Description of job _____

Duties _____

Interviewers (board/manager/personnel officer) _____

B Informal Advice

DEAR JANIS, I'm eighteen years old now but my parents won't let me stay out after ten o'clock at night. All my friends can go home whenever they like, but not me. What can I do? My parents say I'm still not old enough to stay out on my own. I don't want to leave home but I think I'll have to.

A.B. Nottingham.

Dear _____ First of all you'd better think carefully about leaving school. If you stay on two more years you might get a much better job when you leave. Why not try and get a job first? Then, if you get a job, it might be best to talk to your father again. You could tell him you have a good job to go to and it is what you really want to do. Perhaps he'll change his mind. Janis

DEAR JANIS, I'm twenty next birthday and I've got a good job as a librarian. I don't want to live with my mother any more (my father died last year) but she doesn't want me to leave. I feel very sorry for her but I've got my own life to live and I can't stay with her for ever.

M.K. Chester.

DEAR _____ Why not sit down with your parents and have a long serious talk with them? It might be a good idea to show them or persuade them that you are responsible. Tell them that you don't go out alone but with friends. If I were you, I'd let them meet your friends so they can see you are all sensible young people. Janis

DEAR _____ Your situation is very difficult. It might be best to do things very slowly. Why not tell your mother you're going to move out sometime soon so she can get used to the idea? It might be a good idea to stay another six months or so at least because she is obviously still worried about living on her own. You may find then she feels happier about your leaving. Janis

DEAR JANIS, I'm sixteen in August and I want to leave school but my dad says I must stay on till I'm eighteen. I don't want to study any more. I want to get a job and earn some money. What can I do to persuade him?

C.L. Swansea.

1. Read the problem letters and the replies from Janis. Which answer goes with which letter? Write the correct initials in each answer. Then underline the phrases in the answers that are used to offer advice.

2. Work in groups. Do you think Janis gives good advice? If not, what advice would you give?

3. These people are friends of yours. What advice would you give them?

1 _____

2 _____

3 _____

4 _____

5 _____

4. Write down two problems that you have. (If you don't have any problems at the moment, make two up!) Now form groups. Take it in turns to read out your problems and listen to advice from the other members of the group.

C Formal Advice

1. Listen to the conversation once and answer these two questions.

Who are the two people speaking?
What is the problem?

2. The bank manager makes five suggestions. Listen to the conversation again and fill in the blanks below.

_____	not to increase your overdraft.
_____	to take legal action.
_____	asking your solicitor.
_____	you won't increase your overdraft.
_____	pay Reading Chemicals a visit.

3. Mr Hughes is a management consultant. He has just inspected Mr Lloyd's company. He wrote down a few notes while he was inspecting the company. What do you think he said to Mr Lloyd?

Example: *I would advise you to reduce your bank loan.*

- bank loan - enormous
- not many products made
- not enough shops buy the product
- products only sold in Britain
- products not well-made
- prices too high
- staff need incentives
- no staff canteen
- staff inefficient
- too many managers

4. Roleplay: divide into As and Bs. As work in pairs and Bs work in pairs.

Pair A

You are an experienced small shopkeeper. You are going to talk to someone who is interested in starting their own business. He/she wants to start a small newspaper and sweet shop. He/she has no experience and wants your advice. Think about the following points:

★ what to sell — newspapers/magazines/sweets/tobacco etc.
★ how many staff to employ
★ how much to pay them
★ what staff facilities to provide
★ when to open
★ anything else that might be important

Pair B

You are interested in starting a small newspaper and sweet shop but you have no experience of this sort. You are going to talk to an experienced small shopkeeper. Think of all the things you will want to ask him or her about. Look at the list below.

★ what to sell
★ how many staff to employ
★ How to arrange the inside of the shop
★ where to borrow money from
★ how much money you'll need to start
★ anything else you think might be important

Prepare what you will say.
Now make new pairs (one A and one B in each pair) and act out the conversation.

Consolidation

Agony Aunt

IN THE multicultural Britain of today, Nira Sharma has one of the most difficult jobs of all. She writes an agony column for the Indian weekly publication Pavilion. Every day she receives hundreds of letters from people all over the country. These people, of both British and Indian origin, ask her for advice about the problems that arise in their lives from the meeting of two enormously different cultures. She gets a lot of letters from young people. Life is especially difficult for them. They are a part of traditional British culture at school and learn the British way of life. Then after school, they go home and become a part of traditional Indian culture and learn the Indian way of life.

'One of the most difficult problems is marriage', says Mrs Sharma. 'According to Indian tradition all marriages are arranged by the parents. British boys and girls, however, are free to choose who they want to marry. Young British Indians have a terrible problem. Their parents want to choose someone for them, but their friends tell them that they should choose their own partner.'

1. Read the article then decide which sentence best summarises it.

1. Britain is a multicultural society.
2. The meeting of two cultures causes many difficult problems.
3. It is difficult for young Indian people in Britain to get married.

2. *Tradition* and *publication* end in *-tion*. How many other English words do you know that end in *-tion*?

Multicultural means 'with *many* cultures'. How many other English words do you know that begin *multi-*?

3. Listen to the recording of the radio programme 'Your Problems' and decide if the following sentences are true or false.

a) Sita is nineteen years old.
b) She is intelligent.
c) She is going to Bristol University.
d) She is getting married to her boyfriend.
e) Gillian should help Sita to run away from home.
f) Gillian ought to talk to some other Indian people.
g) Ved has an English girlfriend.
h) He wants to go back to Bombay.
i) His parents want him to marry an English girl.
j) He wants to marry an Indian girl.
k) His parents haven't met Wendy.
l) His parents are angry with him.

4. Work in groups. Listen again to Ved's problem and decide what you think is the best advice for him.

5. Imagine you are a good friend of Ved's. When you have decided what advice to give him, write him a letter telling him what you think he should do.

Language Summary

ADVICE

Choose appropriate expressions from the box to fill numbers (1) (2) (4) (5) (10) (11) (13) and (14) in the table.

> If I were in your position, I'd ...
> It might be a good idea to ...
> My advice would be to ...
> Why not ...
> I would advise —ing ...
> Why don't you ...
> You'd better ...
> If you follow my advice, you'll ...

Informal (1) _____
 (2) _____
 (3) If I were you, I'd ...
 (4) _____
 (5) _____
 (6) It might be best to ...
 (7) You should ...
 (8) You ought to ...
 (9) I'd recommend —ing ...
 (10) _____
 (11) _____
 (12) I would advise you to ...
 (13) _____
Formal (14) _____

Test

1. Complete the blanks in the dialogues below.

A: Oh, no! My pen's run out!
B: You'd _____ borrow mine.

A: I've got this terrible pain in my leg!
B: Why _____ you see your doctor?

A: What shall I do about this tax form?
B: I'd _____ taking it to your accountant.

A: We need £10,000 to open a new factory.
B: Well, if you _____ my _____ you'll talk to your bank manager.

A: I haven't been paid for two months.
B: If I _____ in _____, I'd talk to the union.

2. Are the following statements appropriate or inappropriate?

a) You are having great difficulty getting the top off a bottle of lemonade. Your friend says, 'Why not put it under the hot tap?'

b) You are talking to your bank manager about taking out a bank loan. He says, 'My advice would be to borrow as little money as possible'.

c) You come home late with a friend and you don't want to wake up your flatmates. You say to him/her, 'If you follow my advice, you'll take your shoes off'.

d) Your doctor has been unable to cure your migraine. He says, 'I'd recommend seeing a specialist'.

e) A close friend asks for advice about the best and cheapest way to get to Edinburgh. You say, 'If I were in your position, I'd travel by coach'.

Student B, C, D data for information gap exercise on page 119.

> **B, C, D etc**
> You are going to advise your friend on how to approach a job interview. First discuss the following points and add to the list any others you think important. Then listen to your friend's description of the job and offer advice.

1. What clothes to wear.
2. What positive points to stress.
3. What questions to ask the interviewer(s).
4. What to do if you get a very difficult question which you can't answer.
5. _____
6. _____
7. _____
8. _____

16

SUMMARY OF CONTENTS

Functional/notional areas	Describing Something in the Past
Language item(s)	A. Past Continuous B. Past Continuous/Past Simple
Topic	Witnessing Events

Describing Something in the Past

Checkpoint   Complete this extract from *Murder at Basketville Towers*. Use: *do, write, inject, arrive, sit, kill, give, lie, play, try,* in the correct past tense. Use some verbs more than once.

Sherlock Holmes and Dr Watson are investigating a murder.

'Well, Watson, everybody's here. All we have to do now is discover the murderer. What _____ you _____' Sherlock Holmes began, 'between 6 o'clock and 11.30 on the night of the 25th, Doctor?'

'Me?' answered Dr Watson in surprise. 'I say, Holmes, how can you possibly ask that? Surely you don't suspect me? I was with you. You remember. You _____ that dreadful violin. I _____ in my usual chair, by the window. I _____ notes on your last case. You know . . . The one about . . .'

'No, no, Watson, not you. I mean Dr Carver here. Well, Dr Carver?'

'Well, as you know, Holmes,' said the doctor, 'Sir Basil's wife sent for me as soon as she found her husband. He _____ on the kitchen floor with a knife through his chest. I _____ to help him when you _____. But there was nothing I could do.'

'Not at all, Dr Carver. There was a great deal you could do. And you _____ it! When we _____ you _____ Sir Basil an injection – an injection that did not save him, but _____ him!'

'Good heavens, Holmes,' cried Doctor Watson. 'How did you know that?'

'Elementary, my dear Watson. I _____ myself with the same substance. If my theory is correct, I should die within five minutes.'

'Good heavens, Holmes! You're a genius!'

A Past Continuous

1. Listen to this conversation between Miss Tuttle and Sergeant Plodd at the desk of Crookham Police Station and complete the Sergeant's notes below. Use the Past Continuous only.

SUSPECT 1: WINDOW CLEANER?
1 The suspect was wearing _____
2 He was _____
3 A bucket _____
4 He _____
5 He _____

SUSPECT 2: MILKMAN?
1 He _____
2 He _____
3 He _____
4 He _____
5 He _____

2. Would you be a good witness? Look at these photographs of a London policeman giving directions to members of the public. Look at each photograph for ten seconds only, then close your books. Write a description of what the policeman and the other people were wearing, and what they were doing in each photograph.

1   2   3

3. When you have written your descriptions, discuss them with a partner and try to add to the information you have. Do not look at the photographs again!
Now form groups of four, discuss again and add more information if possible. Report back to your teacher.

4. Now work in pairs again. Before checking your descriptions against the photographs, discuss the following statements with your partner and say if each is true or false.

In photograph 1:
a) The man was wearing a tie.
b) The policeman was wearing a watch.
c) The man was wearing glasses.
d) The policeman was pointing with his left hand.
e) The man was standing with his hands in his pockets.

In photograph 2:
a) The man was carrying a case.
b) The policeman was pointing with his left arm.
c) The man was wearing black shoes.
d) The policeman was touching the barrier in front of him.
e) The man and the policeman were looking in the same direction.

In photograph 3:
a) The man was wearing overalls.
b) The man and the policeman were looking in the same direction.
c) The policeman was pointing with his right arm.
d) The man was wearing glasses.
e) The man was holding a newspaper.

B Past Continuous and Past Simple

1. Listen to the account of the coach accident and the following telephone conversation. Complete the sketch map of the accident and mark in with arrows the directions of the vehicles involved. Remember that cars drive on the left hand side of the road in England.

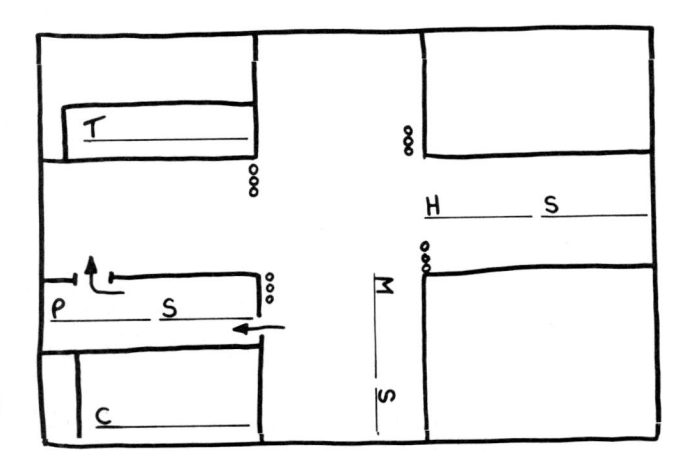

2. Work in pairs, A and B. You both saw the accident and you want to check that you agree about what happened. Look at the notes below and answer the questions with the help of the map you filled in. Note that sometimes you need to use the Past Simple and sometimes the Past Continuous tense.

Example: A: *What was the coach doing?*
B: *It was coming along Market Street.*
B: *How fast ...?*

Notes:
1. What/coach/do?
2. How fast/motorbike/travel?
3. What/motorbike/do wrong?
4. How/coach/avoid/motorbike?
5. What/happen/motorcyclist?
6. What/man in sports car/do?

3. Discuss with your teacher exactly what happened. Do you all agree? Listen to the tape again, if necessary.

4. Complete the following cartoon captions and match them with the correct cartoons. Use the past simple or past continuous of the following verbs as appropriate: *start, win, take, press, come, see, have.*

a) I _____ down the chimney when they _____ to light a fire!
b) He _____ the dog for a walk when it _____ a cat!
c) I don't think my driving instructor has much confidence in me. While I _____ the accelerator, he _____ the brake!
d) I _____ forty-love when we _____ a slight disagreement!

Consolidation

1. A printer has mixed three different stories together in this page of a new book and has forgotten to put in the titles.
   a) Can you separate the three stories? One is about a monster, the second is about an airship and the third is about a famous ship. Find three paragraphs for each story and put them in the correct order. (The first paragraph is in the correct place.)

> A At about 7.30 on a still August evening, Mr Hugh Dyton and his son were working in a field near the loch side.
> B 'I ran over to the side and realised that I was looking at an iceberg. It was so big that it seemed to fill the sky. It was just a few feet away. I felt I could have touched it.'
> C 'The wind was gusting in and the hydrogen was pouring out. We started to sink towards the ground. She was moving slowly forward and pointing her nose downwards.'
> D 'My son was working with me in a field overlooking the loch when he looked up and saw something moving south about half way across the loch. He shouted and the others ran up, and all five of us watched this thing moving down the loch. It was big and black and I realised that after fifteen years of farming here, at last I was actually watching the "Monster" '.
> E 'There was a long rumbling boom like distant thunder. The lights went out, flashed on again, then went out for good. The stern rose until it was pointing almost straight up in the air. Then the liner slipped swiftly and smoothly out of sight.'
> F 'Just as we were nearing the ground a strong gust of wind blew her down hard.'
> G 'The thing was coming down the loch and we could see a long neck coming about six feet out of the water and a head which reminded me rather of a horse, though bigger and flatter. The body was made up of three low humps—about 30-40 feet long and about 4 feet high. It rose up a little out of the water then dived and was gone for good.'
> H 'We pulled away from the liner. The sea was full of wreckage and bodies. Some people had jumped overboard and were screaming for help. The sea was very icy. We wanted to pick them up, but our boat was overloaded already.'
> I 'I heard people in the wreckage crying for help. I was a hundred yards away and the heat was awful. I ran as hard as I could away from that place.'

b) Which photograph belongs to which story?
c) Which of the following titles describes which story: The Airship R101, The Titanic, The Loch Ness Monster?

1

2

3

2. Now check your answers to the reading section by listening to the tape.

3. Now complete the table by filling in all the examples you can find of the Past Simple and Past Continuous tenses in the three stories. (Look back at the reading section in order to do this.)

	LOCH NESS MONSTER	TITANIC	R101
Past Continuous	were working		
Past Simple	Looked up		

Language Summary

Fill in the blanks in the language summary, using words from the box.

| before | completed | continued | describing |
| panicking | simultaneously | unfinished | weren't |

Form:

- The Past Continuous tense is formed by the past tense of the verb *to be* + the present participle.

Affirmative	Negative	Interrogative
I was walking.	I was not/wasn't walking.	Was I walking?
You were walking.	You were not/weren't walking.	Were you walking?
He/she/it was walking.	He/she/it was not/wasn't walking.	Was he/she/it walking?
We/you/they were walking.	We/you/they were not/weren't walking.	Were we/you/they walking?

- *Was not* and *were not* when used informally in speech or writing are contracted to 'wasn't' and _____.
- The verb *to be* can be omitted when used repeatedly after the same subject.
  People were screaming and shouting and generally _____.

Use:

- The Past Continuous tense is used when _____ people, things etc. in the past.
  He was wearing a blue tie.   She was walking very slowly.
  The sports car was doing over 60 miles an hour.
- It is also used when describing _____ actions.
  I was having a bath when the phone rang.
  The phone rang when I was having a bath.

  Here, *I was having a bath* describes an unfinished action, whereas *the phone rang* describes a _____ action.
  It is also possible to have two or more unfinished actions happening _____ in the past.
  I was watching TV while the boys were playing football.
  I was reading the paper, Pete was watching TV and Linda was cooking the meal and listening to the radio.
- When used with a point in time, the Past Continuous describes an action which started before that time and probably continued after it.
  At 10 o'clock I was watching TV.

  This means that you started watching TV _____ 10 o'clock and probably _____ watching for some time afterwards.

Test Complete the following paragraph from a spy story, by using the correct form of the verb in brackets.

Blond (look) _____ in the mirror. (Be) _____ it really him? What (he do) _____ here, anyway? And where (be) _____ 'here'? Russia? What had they done to him? Blond (look) _____ in the mirror again. The face that he (look) _____ at ... (be) _____ it really his? On the other side of the room (be) _____ a woman. She (hold) _____ a gun and (smile) _____. Blond (notice) _____ that she (move) _____ slowly towards him. She (still smile) _____ at him, but the man next to her (not smile) _____. He (play) _____ with a knife. Blond (know) _____ that time (run) _____ out. He would have to act quickly.

'Good evening, Mr Blond.' The girl (lower) _____ the gun and (smile) _____ at him again. 'We (wonder) _____ if you would recognise your new face, weren't we, Tony? You remember us, don't you, James? Reagan and Johnson, CIA. We have a little business together in East Berlin!'

17

SUMMARY OF CONTENTS

Functional/notional areas	Progress and Completion
Language item(s)	A. Present Perfect Simple (Progress) B. Present Perfect Simple (Completion)
Topic	Practical Problems

Progress and Completion

Checkpoint Complete the following, using the word(s) in brackets and putting each verb into the correct tense.

David Boreman is commentating on the 1988 Australian Games.

Good afternoon, and welcome to the Wogawoga Games where we're at a very interesting stage in the final round of the boomerang throwing competition. We __(see/already)__ some excellent throwing. At the end of the fifth round the position is as follows: Klaus Werfer, the East German __(already/go)__ into the lead with a throw of 70 metres 83. The American, Tex Spears __(just/equal)__ the USA record and is in second place with 70 metres 28. Surprisingly, the Russian, Igor Tchukitov __(not throw)__ very well so far today and is in third place. The Australian, Bruce Carter __(be)__ rather unlucky up to now. He threw his boomerang ten minutes ago and it __(still/not come back)__.

But now it's the turn of our own champion, Nigel Peters. He's running up to the line now – Oh! What a lovely action . . . But . . . Wait a minute . . . What's happening? He's lying on the ground holding his head. I think something __(just/hit)__ him! The East German, Werfer, is looking very angry. He's going over to the Australian champion and . . . Oh! He __(push)__ him over! Werfer thought he had won, but he __(not win/yet)__. That's why he was angry. It was Bruce Carter's boomerang that hit Nigel Peters. Oh, and now all the other competitors are fighting. We __(not see)__ scenes like this since Tchukitov was disqualified last year for throwing a hollow boomerang. And, I think . . . Yes . . . The judge is disqualifying all of them! All of them except Nigel Peters who __(still/not move)__. A sad day for the games, but a proud day for Britain and a gold medal for Nigel Peters!

A Present Perfect Simple (Progress)

1. Archaeologist Peter Turner has found an old, wrecked ship near the English coast. Tessa Hunt is interviewing him. Listen to the tape and put a tick (✓) in the table below to show what Peter and his team have done so far.

ITEM	Located	Recovered	Cleaned	Prepared for exhibition
Plates, dishes, cutlery, etc.				
Gold coins				
Cannons				
Royal documents				
Navigation instruments				
Casks of rum/whisky				

2. Work in pairs, A and B. It is one month after the radio interview.

A
You are a newspaper reporter. Ask about progress so far on the *Rose Marie*. Tick the boxes in the table according to the answers, to show what progress has been made.

B
You are an archaeologist working on the *Rose Marie*. Tick the boxes in the table below to show what has happened since last month. It is for you to decide how much progress has been made, but nothing is ready for the exhibition yet, so do not put any ticks in the 'Prepared for exhibition' box. Tell A when you are ready to answer questions.

ITEM	Located	Recovered	Cleaned	Prepared for exhibition
Plates, dishes, cutlery, etc.	✓	✓	✓	

A *How far have you got with the plates, dishes, cutlery and so on?*
B *Well we've located them, recovered them and cleaned them, but we haven't prepared them for exhibition yet/still haven't prepared them for exhibition.*
A *Have you cleaned the gold coins yet?* etc.

3. Use the ticks you have put in the table to help you write a summary of progress so far. Add extra information about the items found if you wish.

> Progress Report on the Rose Marie Project
> There has been good progress so far on the excavation of the Rose Marie.
> 1 They have located, recovered and cleaned some very interesting plates, dishes, cutlery, etc.
> 2 They have...

Now make notes on what the team has not done. Use *still* and *yet*.

Example: 1. *They haven't prepared the plates etc. for exhibition yet.*
They still haven't ...

B Present Perfect Simple (Completion)

1. Listen to the extracts from radio programmes and complete the sentences below. Use the verb in brackets and *just* or *already* as appropriate.

a) *(find)* Archaeologists working on the *Rose Marie* _____ _____ _____ some very important documents.
b) *(come back)* James Hunter _____ _____ _____ _____ from the New Art Exhibition at the Tate.
c) *(retire)* Five drivers _____ _____ _____ from the race with engine problems. Lafitte *(pass)* _____ _____ _____ Mansell.

2. Work in pairs, A and B. Do the 'word race' separately. Complete the compound nouns.

Example:
A: *How many have you done?*
B: *I've done two. I've just finished number 2. How many have you done?*
A: *I've already done five.*

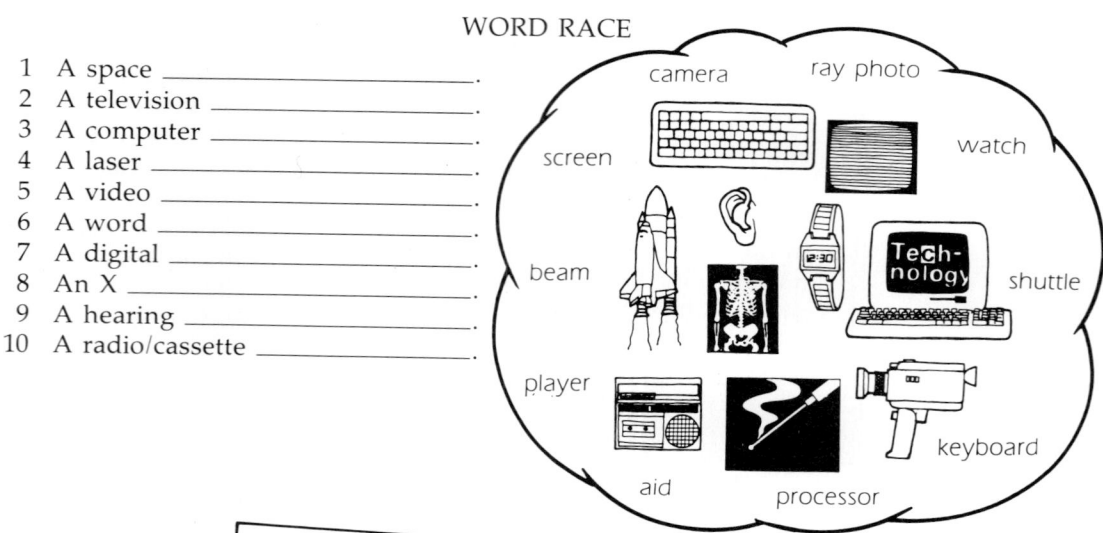

WORD RACE

1 A space _____.
2 A television _____.
3 A computer _____.
4 A laser _____.
5 A video _____.
6 A word _____.
7 A digital _____.
8 An X _____.
9 A hearing _____.
10 A radio/cassette _____.

Technology: camera, ray photo, screen, watch, beam, shuttle, player, keyboard, aid, processor

3. Mr and Mrs Hardy and their three children are on holiday in Spain. Mrs Hardy's postcard got wet in the rain. Can you rewrite it? Use the Present Perfect tense and *already*.

COSTA DEL SOL

We've ___ here five days al___ and so far it ___ every day. Costa del Sol? Costa del Wind and Rain, more like! W___ in the hotel all the time up to now. We've ___ every card game we know and I ___ all the books I brought with me. Otherwise we're having a lovely time and George ___ definitely dec___ he wants to come again next year!
Bye for now, Mandy

Hotel Exotica
Costa Del Sol

Kathy Wigmore
10 Hoveden Road
Sandford
Merseyside
England

Consolidation

1. You are doing a survey for the magazine *Which Garage?*. You have taken three different cars with the same faults to three different garages for repairs. Listen to these telephone conversations and tick (✓) the items in the table below which the garage says needs attention. (You will hear information on only two of the three garages.)

WHICH GARAGE? CHECKLIST			
		Garage	
Item	Denton's	Parker's	Robson's
1. 5,000 mile service			
2. Mend puncture in spare wheel			
3. Adjust handbrake			
4. Put new bulb in front light			
5. Put on new exhaust			
6. Replace gearbox			
7. Adjust steering			
8. Repair radiator			

2. Work in pairs.

A
You need information about the Fiesta from B, who works at Robson's Garage. Telephone B, and tick the item in the box under Robson's, according to the information you receive.

B
You work in the workshop at Robson's Garage. First put a tick in the box under Robson's against those items which you have decided need attention. (You may decide that all or only some of the items need attention.) Now give A the information about what you have done to his or her car. Use the Present Perfect tense and *still, yet, just, almost,* etc.

Example:
A: *Hallo? Is that Robson's?*
B: *Yes, Robson's here. Can I help you?*
A: *My name's _____. Is my Fiesta ready yet?*

3. You now have all the information you need about the three garages, but before you leave the office, your boss asks you to write him a memo about progress so far. Complete the memo.

MEMO

From: _____   Date: _____
To: _____

Subject: Garage Investigation

Progress so far:

1 Denton's: Denton's have done a 5,000 mile service and mended the puncture in the spare wheel. They haven't . . .
2 Parker's
3 Robson's

4. Work in pairs.
You and a colleague work for a television company. You are discussing progress so far on a TV programme called *In the News*. You have some information and your colleague has the rest.

A
Look at the checklist below, ask your colleague (B) for the missing information and write it down.

B
Look at the checklist on page 140 and give the information your colleague asks for. Use the Present Perfect tense when you speak. Do not look at your colleague's checklist.

Have you checked what time the programme begins?

Yes, I've already done that. She's agreed. Have . . .

No, I haven't done that yet. Have you arranged an interview with the Prime Minister about the spy story?

1.	Check what time the programme begins.	Not done yet
2.	Arrange interview with Prime Minister about spy story.	Already done, Agreed
3.	Phone Russian Embassy to arrange interview with Vladimir Kronsky.	Just done. Refused
4.	Ask Russian specialist from Cambridge to comment on situation.	
5.	Complete research on Kronsky.	Nearly completed
6.	Submit list of questions to Prime Minister.	
7.	Check script with legal department.	Still not done

Language Summary

Fill in the blanks in the language summary.

> completed   interrogative   negative   quite   up to now   far   just   present   still   yet

Form

The Present Perfect tense is formed with the present tense of the verb *to have* + the past participle: *I have finished. They have not started.*

For informal speaking and writing the short forms are often used: *I've finished. They haven't started.*

AFFIRMATIVE	NEGATIVE
I have (I've) finished.	I have not (haven't) finished.
_____ (you've) finished.	You _____ not (have) finished.
He/she/it has (he/she/it _____) finished.	He/she/it has not (_____) finished.
We _____ (_____'ve) finished.	We have not (_____).
You (pl.) have (you _____) finished.	You (pl.) _____ not (_____) _____.
They _____ (they've) _____.	They have not (_____) finished.

INTERROGATIVE	
Have __I__ finished?	
_____	
_____	
_____	
_____ we	
_____	
_____	

Use:

(You can use the words in the box to fill the blanks.)
We can use the Present Perfect tense to describe past events that are linked in some way to the _____. For example, in the following ways:

- We use it to describe events that have started in the past, but are not _____ – i.e. to describe progress. We often use it with words (time adverbials) such as *still/yet/nearly/almost/not quite/so far/up to now* etc.

I've nearly finished.
Have you phoned Tom _____?
I've had eight driving lessons so _____.

Position of adverbials
Note that:
- *still* is placed before the verb and is mostly used in _____ sentences.
  He _____ hasn't arrived.
- *yet* is placed at the end of the clause or sentence and is used in negative and _____ sentences.

He hasn't arrived yet.
Have you finished yet?

- *nearly/almost/not quite* are placed after the main part of the verb, but before the past participle.

He's nearly done it.
We've almost arrived.
We haven't _____ finished.

- *so far* and *up to now* are placed either at the beginning (for emphasis) or at the end of the clause or sentence.

Nobody has arrived so far.
So far nobody has arrived.
The police haven't found anything up to now.
_____ the police haven't found anything.

- We use the Present Perfect tense to describe events in the past that have recently been completed.

Have you seen my pen? I put it down there ten minutes ago. Oh! It's all right. I've found it.

We often use words (time adverbials) such as *just/already* in this way.

Position of adverbs

- *just* and *already* are placed after the main part of the verb, but before the past participle:

We've _____ had a phone call from Paris.

A: Do you want any help with the washing up?
B: It's OK. I've already done it.

NB For further uses of the Present Perfect see Language Summary, Unit 18.

Student B data for information gap exercise on page 138.

1	Check what time the programme begins.	Not done yet
2	Arrange interview with Prime Minister about spy story.	Already done She's agreed
3	Phone Russian Embassy to arrange interview with Vladimir Kronsky.	
4	Ask Russian specialist from Cambridge to comment on situation.	Still not done
5	Complete research on Kronsky.	
6	Submit list of questions to Prime Minister.	Just done
7	Check script with legal department.	

Test   Complete this letter to a friend in New York.

17, Stanton Road,
London SW8 6ZZ
England

7th October 19___

Dear Pete,

    Hi! I'm writing to you from London. I _____ (just enrol) on a two month course at the Rex School of English. I _____ (already make) a lot of friends and up to _____ everybody _____ (be) really friendly. One problem, though. I lost one of my cases on the flight over. I rang the airport again this morning, but they _____ (still not find) it. I _____ (ring) them six times so _____ and I'm beginning to think it's lost forever!

    Do you know London? I _____ (not yet visit any of the tourist attractions) _____. It _____ (rain) every day so _____ and I _____ (almost give up) hope that it will ever stop.

    Well, I have to stop now. I _____ (almost finish) my English homework but not _____! Oh, I know what I can do! This letter can be my homework!

    Bye for now. Write soon!

18

SUMMARY OF CONTENTS

Functional/notional areas	Duration
Language item(s)	A. Present Perfect Simple/Past Simple B. For/since/ago
Topic	Studying

Duration

Checkpoint Read this letter from Franz to his Australian friend, Arlene, and correct the Past and Present Perfect tenses where necessary.

17, Wellbeck Street,
Oxford
England
20th November

Dear Arlene,
Hi! Sorry I didn't write for so long. I bet you're surprised to get a letter from me — particularly one with a British stamp! I've arrived in England three days ago, and I'll be here for three weeks. Did you ever visit England? I was here once before in 1983. Then I've stayed in Cambridge since a week and now I'm in Oxford — the other old university town. As I said, I was only here since three days, but already I'm having problems! When the plane arrived at Heathrow I haven't been able to find my luggage. Nobody knows where it is! Maybe someone has put it on the wrong plane at Frankfurt airport when I left. Anyway, I've spent the whole morning at Heathrow filling in forms — that was about three days ago — and I still didn't hear anything about it. Not a very good start! I'll write again soon — with better news, I hope.
Best wishes
Franz

A Present Perfect Simple/Past Simple

1. We often begin a conversation in the Present Perfect tense with no specific time reference. Then we continue by using the Past tense to refer to a specific time.

Example:
- A *Have you ever applied for a place at Oxford University?*
- B *Yes, I have.*
- A *When did you apply?*
- B *Two months ago.*

OR:
- A *Have you applied for a place at Oxford?*
- B *Yes, I have. I applied two months ago.*

Work in pairs. With your partner ask and answer questions, and complete the questionnaire with your partner's answers. Fill in the 'yes/no' column and add any further information in note form. (When you use the Past tense, begin with question words such as *when, where, who,* **etc.)**

	QUESTIONNAIRE Yes/No	Further Information
1 (take) a driving test		
2 (go) skiing		
3 (be) at a pop concert		
4 (meet) an American		
5 (miss) a plane/train		
6 (sing) in the bath		
7 (feel) depressed		
8 (fail) an exam		
9 (lose) your temper		
10 (see) a ghost		

2. Clare Stanton and Alan Hunter have both applied for a place at a college at Oxford University. Listen to Clare's interview first and make a list of all the questions the interviewers ask her in this table, according to which tense is used.

Clare Stanton's Interview

Questions in Present Perfect Tense	Questions in Past Tense
1 _____	1 _____
2 _____	2 _____
3 _____	3 _____
4 _____	
5 _____	

3. Now complete these notes. You will need them later for a discussion. At the end of the notes write down your impression of Clare.

NOTES

Clare Stanton

1. _____ decided which language to specialise in.
2. Has _____ to Germany, but _____ with an English friend and _____ _____ much German.
3. _____ read very much German — except Kafka (possibly)
4. _____ on a course at the Sorbonne last summer
5. _____ _____ all the works of Baudelaire

General impression:

4. Now listen to Alan Hunter's interview. Make a list of all the questions the interviewers ask him on the table below, according to which tense is used.

Alan Hunter's Interview

Questions in Present Perfect Tense	Questions in Past Tense
1 _____	1 _____
2 _____	2 _____
3 _____	
4 _____	

5. Now complete these notes. You will need them later for a discussion. At the end of the notes write down your general impression of Alan.

NOTES

Alan Hunter

1. Has _____ to France and Germany. _____ to Germany year before last (1 month). _____ to Paris last summer.
2. German teacher _____ _____ retire suddenly — may explain low 'A' level mark.
3. _____ read much German literature apart from set books
4. Probably _____ read any French mediaeval literature either.
5. Seems to know more about French Existentialists. _____ read quite deeply here?

General impression:

6. Work in pairs. Clare Stanton and Alan Hunter are competing for the last place at the college. The interviews have just finished. You were one of the interviewers. Look back at your notes, compare them with your colleague, and decide who should have the place, and why. (Use the Present Perfect and Past tenses as much as possible.)

A: OK. Let's look at Clare first. She hasn't decided which language to specialise in.
B: Yes, that's right, but she's been to Germany.
A: But she went with an English boyfriend, so she didn't speak much German. That's not very useful.

When you have finished pair work, discuss with the class as a whole who should have the place. Take a vote if necessary!

7. Write a note to Professor Thomson recommending one of the candidates for the last place at this Oxford college, giving reasons. (Use the Present Perfect and Past tenses as much as possible.)

B For/since/ago

1. Read the description of Merton College, Oxford. As you read, find words in the text to fill these gaps.

started = f_____,   famous = il_____,   private/separate = s_____,
about 400 = s_____ 400,   live = s_____ i_____ r_____,
all three years = t_____ f_____ t_____ y_____.

> ### Merton College, Oxford
>
> Merton College, Oxford, was founded over 700 years ago in 1264 by Walter de Merton, 'Chancellor of the illustrious lord, Henry, King of England' (King Henry III). It is the oldest college in Oxford and is situated in the east part of the town in a quiet and secluded position.
>
> For many years the college specialised in mathematics and science, and it has the oldest library in England, parts of which date from 1371. The library contains over 40,000 volumes and the number is increasing each year.
>
> Merton also possesses a fine garden, unfortunately not open to the public, and nearby, originally built some 400 years ago, is the tennis court where Royal Tennis (the earliest version of tennis) was played. Edward VII played there as Prince of Wales, and the game has in fact been played at Oxford since 1450.
>
> The college admits only about 75 men and women undergraduates each year and is quite small, although it also has about 80 graduates and 50 fellows (professors, researchers, teachers of undergraduates).
>
> Because it is not very large, students are able to stay in residence at the college for the full three years of their degree course if they wish. In most other colleges residence is possible for only one (the first) year and students take lodgings in town for the remainder of their course.
>
> Since its foundation, many famous men have passed through the college, including William Harvey, Lord Randolph Churchill and T.S. Eliot.

2. Complete the following statements. Do not look back at the passage.

a) Merton College was founded over 700 years _____.
b) _____ many years the college specialised in mathematics and science.
c) The library was originally built some 400 years _____.
d) Royal Tennis has been played at Oxford _____ 1450.
e) Students are able to stay in residence _____ the full three years of their course.
f) In most colleges residence is possible _____ only one year.
g) Students take lodgings in the town _____ the remainder of their course.
h) _____ its foundation, many famous men have passed through the college.

Now look back at the passage, check your answers and do this exercise.

i) *since* is used with
 (i) only the Past tense.
 (ii) only the Present Perfect tense.
 (iii) both the Past and Present Perfect tenses.

j) *ago* is used with
 (i) only the Past tense.
 (ii) only the Present Perfect tense.
 (iii) only the Past and Present Perfect tenses.

k) *for* is used with
 (i) only the Past tense.
 (ii) only the Present Perfect tense.
 (iii) both the Past and Present Perfect tenses.

l) Does the passage use *for* with another tense?

m) True or false?
 (i) We use *since* when we refer to a period of time.
 (ii) We use *for* when we refer to a point in time.
 (iii) We use *ago* when we refer to a period of time.

Consolidation

1. The headmaster of Kingsbridge Secondary School is giving an end of term report to the governors of the school. Listen and complete the table below with the correct figures.

	Number of students applying for university places	Number of students accepted	Number of students accepted at Oxbridge
Year before last			
Last year			
This year*			

*Figures are provisional

2. Work in pairs, A and B. As look at the table below; Bs at the table on page 148. The tables refer to six schools and the number of successful university applications made.

Number of Successful University Applications		
School	Last Year	This Year*
1 Queensway	22	18
2 Bishopsridge		
3 Monkton	13	4
4 Knightsgrove		
5 Lordleigh	25	32
6 Earlsbridge		

*Figures are provisional

Example:
A: *How many successful applications were there for Bishopsridge last year?*
B: *Twenty-one.*
A: *And how many have there been so far this year?*

3. Look at the following graph and the report. The information on the graph is correct, but there are some mistakes in the report. Underline the mistakes you find.

4. Now write a correct report based on the graph.

EARLSBRIDGE COMPREHENSIVE
No. of A-level passes per year

REPORT

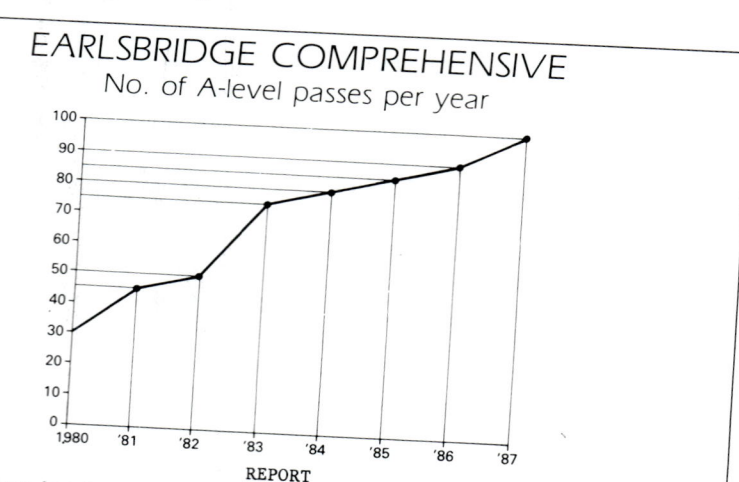

Since 1980 there has been a decline in the number of A level passes. In 1980 there were 90 passes and in 1981 this figure fell to 45. In 1982 there were 44 passes and in 1983 the figures fell again to 22. In 1984 there was a further fall to 20 passes. The fall continued in 1985 (15 passes) and in 1986 (12 passes). Finally, the figures for this year (1987) show that the fall continued until it reached 11 passes - a quarter the number reached five years ago. Clearly, there has been a marked decrease for the last seven years. Seven years ago there were 90 passes, but since then the figures have dropped to less than a quarter of what they were.

Language Summary

Fill in the blanks in the language summary, using the table.

ago	applied	have	past
period	point	present	specific

> PRESENT PERFECT SIMPLE CONTRASTED WITH THE PAST SIMPLE
>
> *Form:*
> See Unit 17, Language Summary, page 139 for rules on the formation of the Present Perfect tense.
>
> *Use:*
> See Unit 17, Language Summary, page 139 for uses of the Present Perfect with time adverbials (*still, yet, just, already,* etc.)
>
> The Present Perfect tense is used to describe past actions that do not have a specific time reference, stated or implied. For specific time references we use the Past Simple.
>
> Non-specific time reference: Have you (ever) been to the USA?
> _____ time reference: When did you visit the USA?
>
> We often begin a conversation in the present perfect tense with no specific time reference. Then we continue by using the _____ tense to refer to a specific time.
>
> A: Have you applied for a place at Oxford University?
> B: Yes, I have.
> A: When did you apply?
> B: Two months ago.
>
> Also, the second speaker may make the change in time focus immediately:
>
> A: _____ you applied for a place at Oxford University?
> B: Yes, I _____ two months ago.
>
> When there is a specific past time reference, the Present Perfect cannot be used. In such cases we use the Past Simple tense:
> I went to Italy last year. (NOT *I have been to Italy last year.*)
>
> We often use the Present Perfect when we are describing a past event that is important to us in the _____ – that is, at the time we are speaking.
>
> I think I've seen this film before!
> Oh, no! I've lost my glasses again.
>
> Note that here, too, no specific past time is stated or implied. We are concerned with the effect of a past action on the present.

FOR/SINCE/AGO

For

For is used with a _____ of time and is used with either the Present Perfect or the Past tense.

I haven't seen him for years.
I waited for twenty minutes, but he didn't come.

Since

Since is used with a _____ in time (e.g. *five o'clock, Christmas, last January, Thursday, 1983,* etc.) and is used with the Present Perfect tense.

I haven't seen him since last Friday.
We've been here since 2 o'clock.

Ago

Ago is used with a period of time and is used with the Past tense. It cannot be used with the Present Perfect tense.

He left five minutes _____.

Student B data for information gap exercise on page 146.

	Number of Successful University Applications	
School	Last Year	This Year*
1 Queensway		
2 Bishopsridge	21	18
3 Monkton		
4 Knightsgrove	24	31
5 Lordleigh		
6 Earlsbridge	19	27

*Figures are provisional

Test

1. Use these notes to write a description of Christ Church College, Oxford. Use the time expressions since, for, ago as much as possible. (Look back at the passage on Merton College if you wish.)

Christ Church College Oxford

1 Was founded in 1525 by Cardinal Wolsey.
2 Then re-founded by Henry VIII in 1532.
3 It is situated near the city centre.
4 It has a cathedral (12th–19th century) and a fine library containing over 100,000 books.
5 Above the main entrance is the famous 'Tom Tower' containing 'Great Tom', a bell made in 1680 that rings 101 times every night at 9.05 p.m. and weighs over six tons.
6 The college admits both men and women — about 120 each year.
7 All undergraduates may spend at least 2 years in rooms in their college.
8 Famous men include C.L. Dodgson (who under the name of Lewis Carroll wrote the famous book 'Alice in Wonderland') and many prime ministers of Britain.

2. Correct this letter from Chantal to her Spanish friend, José.

```
                                    23 Stafford Road,
                                    Hampstead,
                                    London, NW3 4BL
                                    ENGLAND

                                    27th May 19...
Dear José,

    I am here in London since three days now. When
I've arrived at Heathrow it was raining, of course!
I was to England three times before, so I know what
to expect!
    Mr and Mrs Hunter-Jones are very nice, but their
children are terrible! Yesterday, the little one,
Nigel, has thrown his food all over Annabel! Annabel
has screamed so loudly that I think I'm now permanently
deaf. Mrs Hunter-Jones said she would murder both of
them if they didn't behave properly, and since then
there was no more trouble - except yesterday when
Annabel has sat on Nigel 'by mistake' - at least -
she has said it was by 'mistake'
    It's strange to think that only for a week I was
showing you around Paris. Since then so much is
happened. How's life in Madrid? Write soon. I haven't
a letter from you since two days!

                        Love
                           Chantal xxx
```

UNIT 18   149

19

SUMMARY OF CONTENTS

Functional/notional areas	Reason and Purpose
Language item(s)	A. Present Simple Passive B. Asking for Information: expressing reason and purpose
Topic	Science and Knowledge

Reason and Purpose

Checkpoint   Choose the correct words to fill in the blanks in 1 and 2.

1. When the sea __(heat)__ by the sun, the sea water evaporates and rises as water vapour. As the water vapour rises, clouds __(form)__ by condensation. When the clouds reach high land, their temperature falls and rain __(produce)__. The rain __(absorb)__ into the earth and __(carry)__ by streams and rivers until it flows back again into the sea.

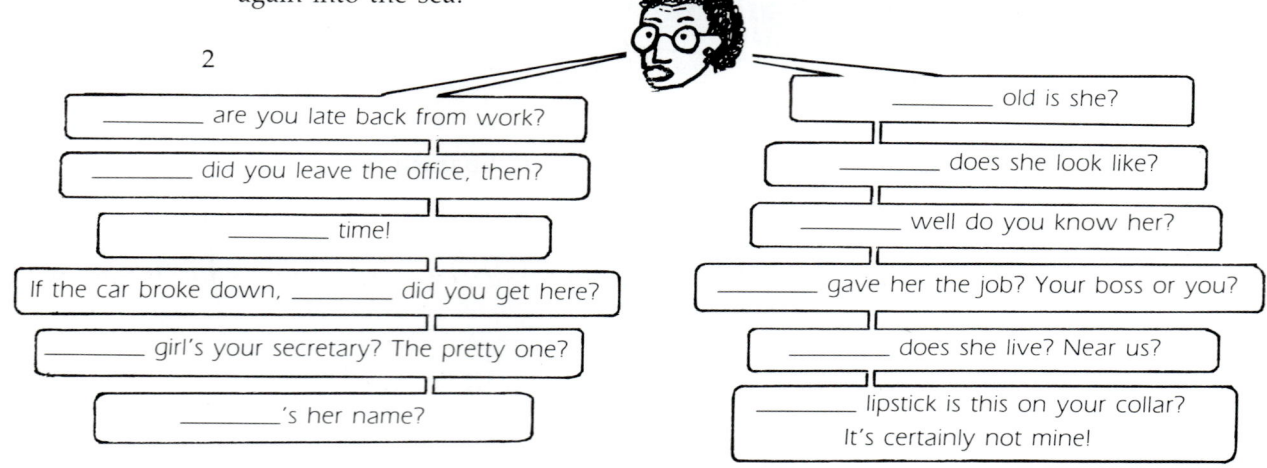

2.
- _____ are you late back from work?
- _____ did you leave the office, then?
- _____ time!
- If the car broke down, _____ did you get here?
- _____ girl's your secretary? The pretty one?
- _____'s her name?

- _____ old is she?
- _____ does she look like?
- _____ well do you know her?
- _____ gave her the job? Your boss or you?
- _____ does she live? Near us?
- _____ lipstick is this on your collar? It's certainly not mine!

3. **Read this conversation and circle the correct word in the brackets.**

Customer   I quite like this recorder. Could you show me how it works?

Shop Assistant   Certainly, miss. You press this button (*because/for/to*) switch it on. OK? And you press this one (*so that/in order that/to*) play.

Customer   I see. And what do I have to do (*so/because of/in order to*) record?

Shop Assistant   Well, you have to press both the play and record buttons (*to/so that/so*) record. You can look at this indicator (*for/so as to/because of*) check that you are, in fact, recording.

Customer   And these? What are these for?

Shop Assistant   Oh, the headphones. They come with the tape recorder (*because of/to/so*) you can listen without disturbing other people.

Customer   That's a good idea. The neighbours are always writing me rude notes (*because/to/because of*) the noise from my stereo ... But listen! It doesn't work! When I press this button nothing happens!

Shop Assistant   That's (*so/because of/because*) I haven't plugged it in yet!

A Present Simple Passive

1. In Britain, all cars over three years old have to be tested for safety. This is called the MOT (Ministry of Transport) test. Listen to the garage owner describing the test, and complete the notes, using the Present Simple Passive.

The MOT Test

First the lighting equipment _____ and the headlamp aim _____.

Then the steering and suspension _____. Then the car _____ onto a 'rolling road' and the brakes _____. The tyres _____ then _____ to make sure they are in good condition, and the wheels _____. Then the seat belts _____ to make sure they're operating efficiently.

The other items, such as windscreen washers and wipers _____, the horn _____ and the exhaust system thoroughly _____. Also the condition of the bodywork _____ for any signs of rust in important structural areas.

The customer _____ then _____ of any faults, any necessary work _____, and the car _____. A test certificate _____ only when all the necessary repairs have been done and the car re-tested.

2. Read through this MOT check-list. Working in turn with your partner make true and false statements about the list and respond to them.

Example: A: *Headlamps are checked under Section VI.*
           B: *No, they aren't/they're not. They're checked under Section I.*

           B: *The horn is tested under Section II.*
           A: *No, it isn't/it's not. It's tested under Section VI.*

Code	Testable item	Code	Testable item
01	Section I – Lighting Equipment	23	Service Brake Efficiency
02	Oblig. Front Lamps	24	Parking Brake Efficiency
03	Oblig. Rear Lamps	25	Service Brake Balance
04	Oblig. Headlamps	25	
05	Headlamp Aim	27	Section IV – Tyres & Wheels
06	Stop Lamps	28	Tyre Type
07	Rear Reflectors	29	Tyre Condition
08	Direction Indicators	30	Roadwheels
09		31	
10	Section II – Steering & Suspension	32	Section V – Seat Belts
11	Steering Controls	33	Security of Mountings
12	Steering Mechanism	34	Condition of Belts
13	Power Steering	35	Operation
14	Transmission Shafts	36	
15	Stub Axle Assemblies	37	Section VI – General Items
16	Wheel Bearings	38	Windscreen Washers
17	Suspension	39	Windscreen Wipers
18	Shock Absorbers	40	Horn
19		41	Condition of Exhaust System
20	Section III – Braking System	42	Effectiveness of Silencer
21	Service Brake Condition	43	Condition of Vehicle Structure
22	Parking Brake Condition	44	

Reproduced with the permission of the Controller of HMSO.

152

B Asking for information

1. Read the newspaper article. Ask your teacher any new words, or use your dictionary. Work on your own or in pairs.

STRANGE red and white lights hovered overhead as three women drove home from their weekly night out.

Mysteriously, their car came to a halt outside the Shamrock cafe on the A5 in Shropshire, though the driver had her foot hard down on the accelerator.

Then the lights suddenly vanished and the trio rushed excitedly to a nearby police station, where they reported a close encounter with a UFO.

But that was when they noticed something even stranger had happened. The drive to the police station should have taken five minutes. Instead, it took twenty-five.

Only now, with the help of hypnosis under the strictest supervision, has an explanation been found for those missing twenty minutes. And it is amazing.

Each of the women has independently told the same story — that they did indeed have a close encounter, far closer than they first imagined. For each says she was taken aboard a spacecraft, examined by alien beings and then released.

Gruff

None of the three had been drinking on that fateful Thursday night. They had all stuck to Coca-Cola. But, although hypnotised separately, they each describe the spaceship and its inhabitants the same way.

They say the ship was steel, circular and brightly lit. They speak of 4ft tall aliens dressed in green, and imitate the spacemen's distinctive gruff voices.

And they have each made similar drawings of what the ship looked like.

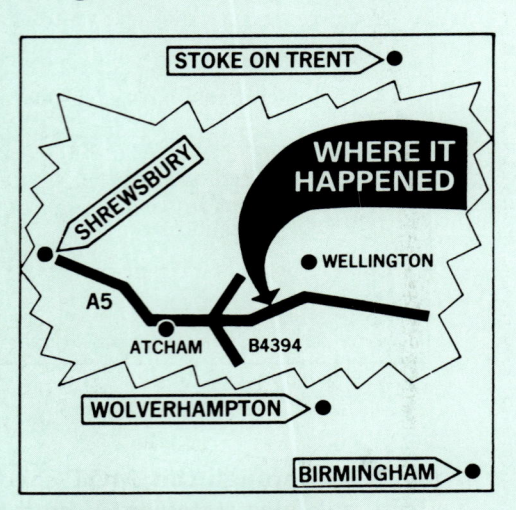

THE SPOT where a UFO captured the women

SPECIAL REPORT

by KEITH BEABEY
and PIPPA SIBLEY

Victims' view of the ship

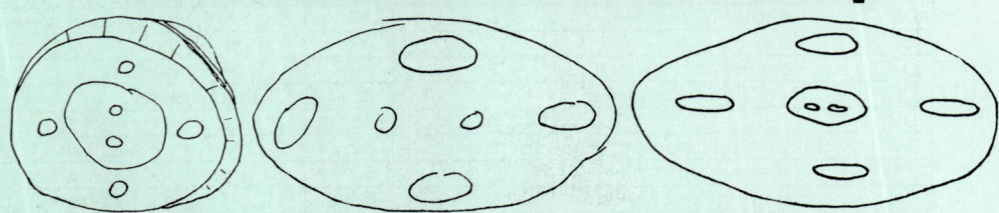

UNCANNY: Under hypnosis the three women produced similar drawings of the spaceship's underside

2. Now make a list of at least ten questions that you think the reporter asked the three women in order to get their story. Use as many different questions as possible.

Example: *What colour were the lights you saw?*
Where had you been?
What did the spaceship look like? etc.

3. Now, in turn, ask your partner your questions and answer his or her questions. Score one point for each correct answer made without referring back to the newspaper article.

4. Two members of your class claim to have seen a spaceship and to have been taken inside. Interview them separately to check that they are telling the truth. Your teacher will give you further instructions.

5. Listen to the interview between a newspaper reporter and an expert on UFO (Unidentified Flying Objects) research, and complete the reporter's notes with words that express reason or purpose. (See Language Summary on page 155.)

NOTES

1 The three women were interviewed separately _____ make sure their stories agreed with each other.

2 The women agreed to be hypnotised _____ all the details could be checked.

3 It wasn't a story that they made up _____ get publicity. This is clear _____ their reactions under hypnosis.

4 Maybe the 'spacemen' came _____ carry out a scientific investigation of some kind.

5 The 'spacemen' erased the women's minds like a tape-recorder _____ they wouldn't remember what happened. But part of their minds was not affected, _____ they were able to remember everything that happened under hypnosis.

Now check your answers with your partner.

Consolidation

1. Work in pairs. Complete the questions in the 'Masterbrain' Quiz, using question words, expressions of purpose and reason, and the following verbs in the passive (note that some verbs are used twice): *eat, burn, visit, play, speak, elect, wear, use, celebrate, know*. Do NOT answer the questions!

MASTERBRAIN

1 <u>Where</u> <u>are</u> kilts <u>worn</u>?
   a) England
   b) Scotland
   c) Wales

2 _____ _____ cricket _____?
   a) Lords
   b) Wimbledon
   c) Wembley

3 _____ _____ turkeys traditionally _____?
   a) at the New Year
   b) at Easter
   c) at Christmas

4 _____ _____ the Queen's official birthday _____?
   a) June 12th
   b) June 13th
   c) June 14th

5 _____ _____ _____ every 5th of November?
   a) Joan of Arc
   b) Guy Fawkes
   c) Archbishop Cranmer

6 Madame Tussaud's is a place which _____ _____ by thousands of people _____ its
   a) fashionable dresses
   b) famous photographs
   c) wax figures

7 _____ _____ the 'best' English _____?
   a) in the North-east
   b) in the South-east
   c) in the Midlands

8 _____ birthplace _____ _____ regularly at Stratford on Avon?
   a) Shakespeare's
   b) Dickens'
   c) Graham Greene's

9 _____ other name _____ the London Underground _____ by?
   a) the metro
   b) the tube
   c) the subway

10 _____ often _____ the British Parliament _____?
   a) every 3 years
   b) every 4 years
   c) every 5 years

11 In Devon (S.W. England) apples _____ _____ _____ make
   a) beer
   b) apple pies
   c) cider

12 Welsh _____ _____ in Wales
   a) because nobody in Wales understands English
   b) so the English can't understand Welsh
   c) to preserve traditions and prevent the Welsh language from dying out

Now check with your teachers that you have completed all the questions correctly. Do NOT answer the questions yet.

2. Work in pairs.

Student A ask Student B all the questions and put a circle round the letters (a, b, c) according to the answers B gives you. Do not write in the boxes. When all the answers have been given, Student B ask Student A all the questions, and circle the appropriate answers in the same way. You each now have a record of your partner's answers.

Example: A: *Where are kilts worn? In England, Scotland or Wales?*

3. Now listen to the final of the Masterbrain competition, and mark your partner's answers. If the answer is correct put a tick in the box. If not, put a cross. If you have all twelve questions right, you have done very well!

4. Now, working together in groups of four, make a questionnaire with eight questions which contain examples of the present passive and expressions of purpose and reason (*because/because of/so/to/*etc.)

Language Summary

Fill the blanks in the language summary, using the words in the box.

because   because of   doer   emphasis   receiver   so as to   that

1 PRESENT SIMPLE PASSIVE

Form
The present simple passive is formed with the present tense of the verb *to be* + the past participle. *By* can be used (although it is often not used) to express the agent or 'doer' of the action.
Example: Kilts are worn in Scotland.
Clouds are formed by condensation.
The aircraft is checked regularly (by the engineers).

Use
The passive is not simply a translation of the active. There is a change of _____ from the doer of an action to the receiver. If we wish to stress that the _____ of the action is more important to us than the _____, we use the passive.
Example: The aircraft is checked regularly.
Here, the important fact is what happens to the aircraft, not who checks it.

2 QUESTION WORDS

The following words are commonly used to start questions: *When, Why, What, Who, Whose, Where, Which, How*. Note that prepositions can precede *what, who* (this becomes *whom*), *whose* and *which*. The language then becomes more formal.
Example 1 For what reason is he here?   3 In whose name is the contract signed?
2 To whom shall I send it?   4 On which train is he arriving?
The use of 'whom' is particularly formal. Informal versions of the formal sentences above are:
1 Why is he here?   3 Who signed the contract?
2 Who shall I send it to?   4 Which train is he arriving on?

3 EXPRESSIONS OF PURPOSE

In order to, so as to, so that, so (The expression *in order that* also exists, but is rather formal)
a) *in order to, so as to* and *to* are followed by an infinitive.
Example:
He opened the window { in order to / _____ / to } let out the smoke.

In order to and *so as to* are a little more formal than just *to*, which is more commonly used in everyday speech and informal writing.

b) *so that* and *so* are followed by a clause.
Example:
He spoke softly { so _____ / so } nobody else could hear.

so is a little more informal than *so that*.

4 EXPRESSIONS OF REASON:

because/because of
because is followed by a clause, _____ by a noun (or noun phrase).
Example: A Why did you leave so early?
B _____ I was tired.
C Because of the guests!
D The conversation was boring!

Test

1. Use the information on the flow chart to complete the description of how a manuscript becomes a book.

FROM MANUSCRIPT TO BOOK

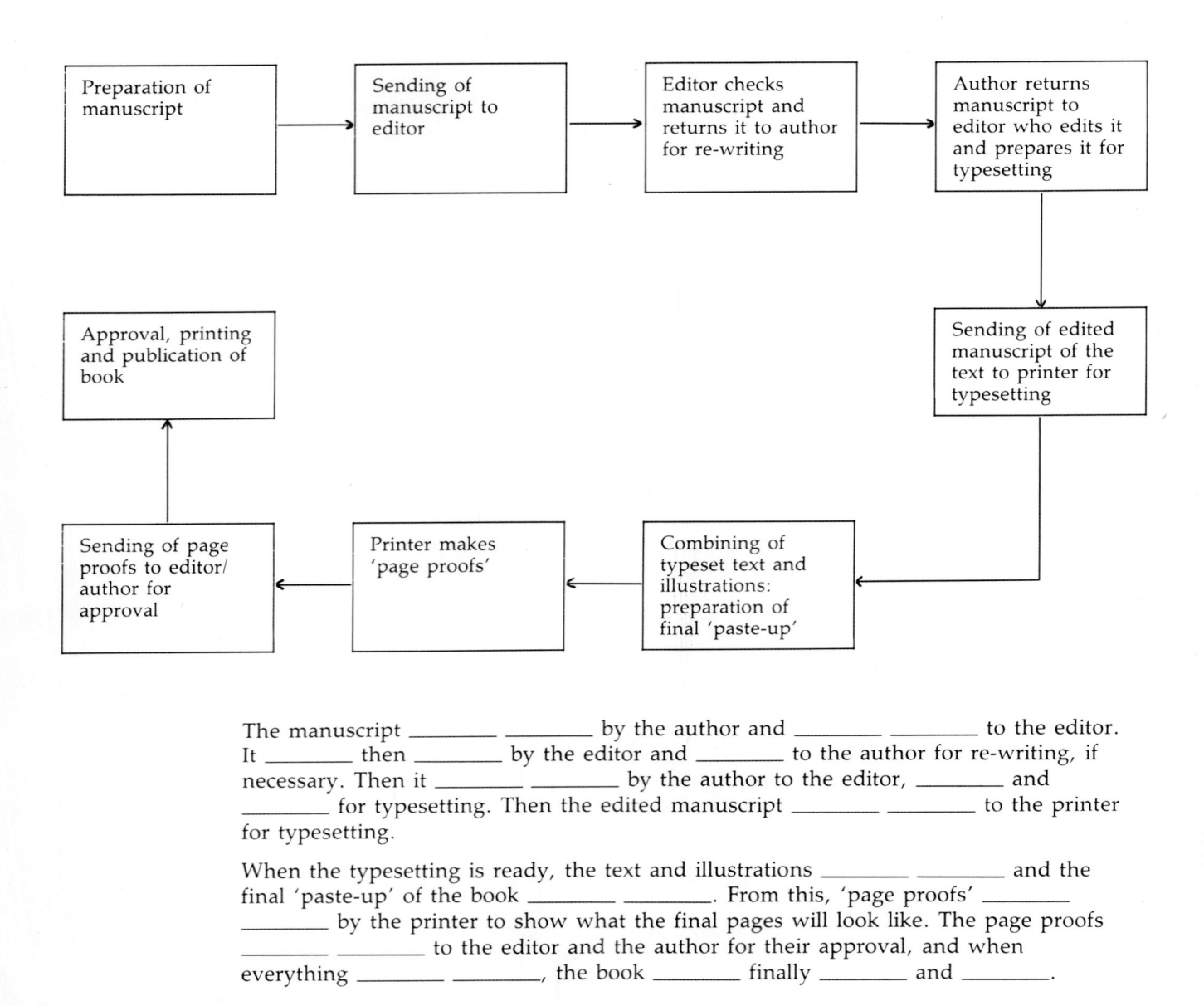

```
┌──────────────┐   ┌──────────────┐   ┌──────────────┐   ┌──────────────┐
│ Preparation  │──▶│ Sending of   │──▶│ Editor checks│──▶│ Author returns│
│ of manuscript│   │ manuscript to│   │ manuscript   │   │ manuscript to │
│              │   │ editor       │   │ and returns  │   │ editor who    │
│              │   │              │   │ it to author │   │ edits it and  │
│              │   │              │   │ for re-writing│  │ prepares it   │
│              │   │              │   │              │   │ for typesetting│
└──────────────┘   └──────────────┘   └──────────────┘   └──────────────┘
                                                                │
                                                                ▼
┌──────────────┐                                          ┌──────────────┐
│ Approval,    │                                          │ Sending of   │
│ printing and │                                          │ edited       │
│ publication  │                                          │ manuscript of│
│ of book      │                                          │ the text to  │
│              │                                          │ printer for  │
│              │                                          │ typesetting  │
└──────────────┘                                          └──────────────┘
       ▲                                                         │
       │                                                         │
┌──────────────┐   ┌──────────────┐   ┌──────────────┐           │
│ Sending of   │◀──│ Printer makes│◀──│ Combining of │◀──────────┘
│ page proofs  │   │ 'page proofs'│   │ typeset text │
│ to editor/   │   │              │   │ and          │
│ author for   │   │              │   │ illustrations:│
│ approval     │   │              │   │ preparation  │
│              │   │              │   │ of final     │
│              │   │              │   │ 'paste-up'   │
└──────────────┘   └──────────────┘   └──────────────┘
```

The manuscript _____ _____ by the author and _____ _____ to the editor. It _____ then _____ by the editor and _____ to the author for re-writing, if necessary. Then it _____ _____ by the author to the editor, _____ and _____ for typesetting. Then the edited manuscript _____ _____ to the printer for typesetting.

When the typesetting is ready, the text and illustrations _____ _____ and the final 'paste-up' of the book _____ _____. From this, 'page proofs' _____ _____ by the printer to show what the final pages will look like. The page proofs _____ _____ to the editor and the author for their approval, and when everything _____ _____, the book _____ finally _____ and _____.

2. A Martian has just landed in your back garden! Make a list of all the questions you can think of to ask him – assuming he speaks English! You should have at least eight different *'wh'* questions.

3. Now the Martian is asking YOU some questions. Answer them, using as many different expressions of purpose and reason as possible.

a) What do you use legs for?
b) Why do you have lungs?
c) What are your glasses for?
d) Why are you wearing clothes?
e) Why are you holding an umbrella?
f) Why are you smoking a cigarette?
g) Why are you shaking?

20

SUMMARY OF CONTENTS

Functional/notional areas	Reporting
Language item(s)	A. Reported Speech – Say/tell/ask B. Reported Speech – Tense Changes C. Reported Speech – Pronoun Changes D. Reported Speech – Adverbials of Time
Topic	Messages, Instructions, Reports

Reporting

Checkpoint

1. Put a tick (✓) if you think the sentences are correct, a cross (✗) if you think they are wrong.

a) He said me to wait.	f) They told me you weren't well.
b) She told that he liked you.	g) We asked if the museum was open on Thursday.
c) He asked can you come.	h) I asked where the station was.
d) He said he spoke English.	i) They said me to come back later.
e) They asked when does the football match start.	j) She asked him where he had been.

2. Read what Arthur Smith said, and complete the newspaper extract below.

   We went on strike for two months last year . . . We've been on strike for six weeks . . . We're still on strike now.

   MR ARTHUR SMITH, leader of one of the country's largest unions, said that the ELTU _____ on strike for two months last year, that they _____ on strike for six weeks, and that they _____ still on strike now.

3. Read the speech bubbles then complete sentences (a) to (d).

   I invited you to my party but you didn't come.
   We didn't get your invitation.

   I posted the letter to you on Friday.
   But you didn't send it first class.

   a) He said _____'d posted the letter to _____ on Friday.
   b) She said _____ hadn't sent it first class.
   c) He said _____'d invited _____ to _____ party, but _____ hadn't come.
   d) They said _____ hadn't got _____ invitation.

4. **Read what the five different people said on April 3rd.**

John: *I'm going on holiday tomorrow.*
Alice: *I didn't get back until last night.*
Mike: *I finished my exams yesterday.*
Albert: *I'm leaving on the 25th.*
Molly: *I haven't seen my brother at all today.*

You are reporting what they said on the different dates shown. Look at the dates and complete the missing words as appropriate.

a) April 4th   John said he was going on holiday _____.
b) April 4th   Mike said he'd finished his exams _____.
c) April 11th   Albert said he was leaving _____.
d) April 8th   Alice said she hadn't got back until _____.
e) April 10th   Molly said that she hadn't seen her brother at all _____.

A Reported Speech — Say, tell, ask

> say (that) ...
> tell someone (that) ...
> tell someone to ...
> ask (someone) to ...
> ask (someone) + wh question word ...
> ask someone if + clause

1. **Listen to Clare Taylor taking her driving test, and complete this part of a letter.**

> First the examiner _____ Clare _____ and she _____.
> They went outside, but Clare couldn't find it. The examiner _____
> Clare again _____ knew _____ was and Clare had to
> _____ didn't. Then the examiner _____ the number-
> plate of another car, but she couldn't even see the car. The examiner
> then _____ short-sighted and _____ she _____
> glasses. Clare _____ she didn't, but the examiner _____
> her she ought to. Then he _____ another number-plate. Clare
> then _____ him _____ number-plate _____
> _____. The examiner _____ her, but she _____ she
> couldn't read it because it was muddy. Then the examiner _____'d
> failed the test and _____ she should go and have an eye-test,
> because she obviously needed glasses. Clare didn't even get
> into the car!

2. **Working first in pairs, then in groups, discuss your completed notes and agree on a final version. Choose a group leader to report back to the class for your group.**

B Reported Speech – Tense Changes

| Present → Past | Past → Past Perfect / Past | Present Perfect → Past Perfect |

Present→Past

1. Read sentences (a) to (h) carefully. Listen to the telephone message. Are the sentences true or false according to the tape?

a) Mr Evans said there were no problems with the CX 25 order.
b) He said Crawfords were on strike.
c) He said Crawfords weren't producing anything at all.
d) He said there was a meeting between the management of Carringtons and the unions on the 27th.
e) He said things looked good.
f) He asked which supplier he should contact.
g) He said Carringtons supplied BX 25s.
h) He said Crawfords usually needed over three weeks' notice before delivery.

Past→Past Perfect/Past

2. Read sentences (a) to (h) carefully. Listen to the next recorded message. Are the sentences true or false according to the tape?

a) Bella said she had gone to a dance.
b) She said she hadn't got back until midnight.
c) She said she'd stayed at a man's house.
d) She said she'd completely forgotten her father had wanted her to bring back his car.
e) She said she'd only remembered at about half past three in the morning.
f) She said she'd parked the car where there were no yellow lines.
g) She said a policeman had given her a ticket.
h) She said the policeman had been quite helpful.

Present Perfect→Past Perfect

3. Read sentences (a) to (h) carefully. Listen to another recorded message. Are the sentences true or false according to the tape?

a) 'Cuddle Puss' is Mr Johnson's other daughter.
b) Their birthdays are at the same time of year.
c) She asked him if he liked her birthday present.
d) She said she had just got his birthday present.
e) She said she'd bought two air tickets for a friend.
f) She said she'd been to Barbados before.
g) She asked if he'd travelled by air before.
h) She said she hadn't definitely decided yet whether to go.

4. Work in pairs. Discuss your answers to all of the true/false statements above, using reported speech (*Yes, he/she said that* ... *No, he/she didn't say there was* ...).

C Reported Speech – Pronoun Changes

1. Chief Fireman Hawkins is instructing some new firemen on how to put out a fire, but he gets confused. Form groups and take the part of either the Chief Fireman, Davis, Johnson or Nash. Repeat again exactly what the Chief Fireman said, so that everything is absolutely clear. Interrupt if you think the person you are talking to has made a mistake.

> Nash, I want you to go round the back, no, wait a minute ... I mean up on the roof. But you're not to do anything until you get my signal, OK?

> Right, Johnson. I want you and Davis to go round to the front ... er ... no ... the back of the house and wait for me and Blagg and Nash ... no, Blagg and Picket, I mean.

Blagg Picket Davis Johnson Nash

Johnson⟶Chief Fireman Hawkins
You said you wanted ...
Then you told Nash you wanted ...
Davis⟶Chief Fireman Hawkins
You said you wanted ...
Then you told Nash you wanted ...
Nash⟶Chief Fireman Hawkins
You said you wanted ...
Then you told ...

Johnson⟶Davis
He said he wanted ...
Then he told Nash ...
Nash⟶Davis and Johnson
He said he wanted ...
Then he told ...
Davis⟶Nash
He said he wanted ...
Then he told ...

2. Everything went wrong! The fire burned down the building and Hawkins is blaming you. Write a report of what you think the instructions were, according to whether you were Chief Fireman Hawkins, Johnson, Nash or Davis.

D Reported Speech – Adverbials of Time

1. You are Mr Baxter's secretary. It is now Monday morning. Listen to the extracts from recorded messages made on Saturday (two days earlier) and write them down.

2. Check with your partner that you have written the same messages. Read them out in turn to each other, and discuss any differences or changes that should be made.

Consolidation

1. Basher Hoskins and Blagger Davis are suspected of robbing a bank. Read Basher's statement carefully. You will need to compare it later with Blagger's account of what happened.

Interview with Basher Hoskins: Tape Transcript

Inspector Hunt	Right, Basher. Where were you last night?
Basher	Me? I was in the Fish and Bucket with Blagger Davis and Jimmy the Cat. We stayed there until closing time. You can check if you like.
Inspector Hunt	We will, don't worry. And where did you go after the pub? Straight home to bed, I suppose?
Basher	No, Jimmy went home, but Blagger and me went for a meal at the Indian Star.
Inspector Hunt	Hot curry, was it?
Basher	Yes. Very hot. Why?
Inspector Hunt	I just wondered. And when did you leave the Indian restaurant?
Basher	About midnight, I think it was. Then we took a taxi to the Blue Flamingo—you know—that new night club.
Inspector Hunt	Oh, yes. I know the one. How much was the fare?
Basher	The fare? Oh, you mean the taxi ... er ... six quid I think it was.
Inspector Hunt	And how long did you spend at the Blue Flamingo?
Basher	Er ... we stayed until about three o'clock. It was great. Then we got a taxi home.
Inspector Hunt	And who paid for the taxi? You or Blagger?
Basher	Er ... I did. It dropped Blagger off first. I got home about half past three in the morning.
Inspector Hunt	All right, Basher. That's all ... for the moment. I'm going to have a little chat with your friend, Blagger.

---

2. Now listen to Inspector Hunt's interview with Blagger Davis. Note down any differences that you hear. You will need your notes later to write a report.

3. Discuss your answers in groups of four. How many differences between the two stories could you find?

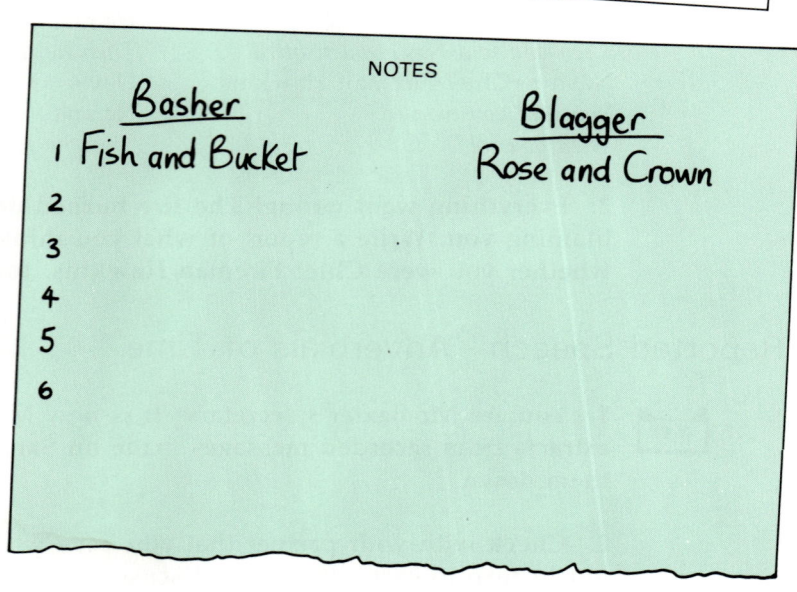

NOTES

Basher	Blagger
1 Fish and Bucket	Rose and Crown
2	
3	
4	
5	
6	

4. Now write your report, using your notes to help you.

Language Summary

Fill the gaps in the language summary, using the words in the box.

| before | 'd | didn't | her | if | indirect | on | question | that | to | us |

1 INTRODUCTORY WORDS

say (that) ...
Say is followed by a clause construction. If *say* is followed by *that* the sentence is more formal than if *that* is omitted. Notice that *say* is never followed by an object pronoun. We can't say: *He said me* etc. although it is possible to use an indirect pronoun with *to: What did he say to you?*

Examples: He said he would be late. (informal)
He said _____ he would be late. (formal)

tell (someone) that ...
Tell is followed by a clause construction and must be followed by an indirect object (pronoun, noun, etc.). We cannot say: *He told that* etc.

Examples: He told her/Linda he couldn't wait. (informal)
He told _____/Linda *that* he couldn't wait. (formal)

tell (someone) to ...
Tell is followed by an indirect object, plus an infinitive construction. We cannot use the infinitive alone: *He told to* etc.

Examples: He told us/everybody to leave immediately.
They told him _____ wait outside.

ask (someone) to ...
Ask can be followed by an infinitive construction which may or may not be preceded by an _____ object.

Examples: He asked to see the manager.
He asked me to visit him in Paris.

ask (someone) + wh question words
Ask can be followed by *wh* question words. Note that in indirect speech we do not invert the subject and verb. We cannot say: *He asked who were you talking to?* Our reported sentence is a statement, not a question ... Therefore we do not invert the subject and verb as we would for a _____. We can say *Who are you talking to?*, but we report this as *He asked who you were talking to*. (The subject and the verb are not inverted.)

Examples: He asked (me) when you were coming.
She asked (Tony) why you hadn't written for so long.

ask (someone) if + clause
Ask can be followed by an optional indirect object, plus *if*, plus a clause, when sentences that begin with a verb are reported.

Examples: 'Are you Mr Johnson?'
He asked (me) if I was Mr Johnson.
'Do you speak English?'
She asked (them) _____ they spoke English.

2 TENSE CHANGES

*Note that in this and all the following sections on reported speech, it is assumed that we are not reporting speech *immediately after* the actual words were spoken. This is covered in Book 2, and entails using the introductory reporting verb in the present tense with no change in the main verb, for example, *He says he can't come.* Book 2 also deals with the common practice of using 'summarising verbs' for reporting, such as *admit, deny, agree, suggest,* etc.

Present→Past
When the Present Simple tense is used in direct speech, it is normally reported in the Past Simple. However, if the reported information is true for the present, it is also possible for it to be reported in the Present.

Example: 'I don't like Peter.'
He said he _____ like Peter. (Those were his feelings at the time.)
He said he doesn't like Peter. (And those are still his feelings now.)

Past→Past Perfect/Past
When the Past Simple tense is used in direct speech, it can be reported either in the Past Perfect, or in the Past Simple without any change. If the Past Perfect is used, the emphasis is on the reporting more than the facts themselves.

Example: Peter arrived late.
They said Peter had arrived late. (Emphasis on reporting.)
They said Peter arrived late. (Emphasis simply on the past fact.)

Present Perfect→Past Perfect
When the Present Perfect tense is used in direct speech, it is reported in the Past Perfect.

Example: 'I've lost my keys.'
He said he had (he _____) lost his keys.

3 PRONOUN CHANGES

Note that pronouns may require changing in order to convey the same meaning as intended in the direct speech.

Examples: *Peter:* 'I told you to be quiet!'
Peter told me/you/him/us/them to be quiet.
(Peter is speaking to Linda and Annabel.)
Peter: 'I'll take you to a disco on Saturday.'
(Later, Annabel is reporting what Peter said to Nigel.)
Peter said he'd take _____ to a disco on Saturday.

4 CHANGES IN ADVERBIALS OF TIME

Note that adverbials of time may require changing in order to convey the same meaning as intended in the direct speech.

Example: 'I'll see you tomorrow.'
Tessa said she'd see me today/yesterday/the day _____ yesterday/on Tuesday/_____ the third ... etc.
The time adverbial chosen depends on exactly when the reporting is taking place.

Test

1. Correct sentences (a) to (f).

a) She told that she like you.
b) They asked where was London Street.
c) He said me he spoke English.
d) They asked did you play tennis.
e) He asked me that I come tomorrow.
f) They told him be here at six o'clock.

2. Report Tessa's statement.

Tessa: *I didn't like him when I met him and I don't like him now. I've never liked him.*

Tessa said she _____

3. Complete the following sentences according to who is reporting.

[Illustration: Pete asks "Did you have a good holiday, you two?" Cathy and Tom reply "Yes, it was great."]

Tom   Pete asked _____ if _____'d had a good holiday, and Cathy told _____ it had been great.

Cathy   Pete asked _____ if _____'d had a good holiday and _____ said it had been great.

Pete   _____ asked them if _____'d had a good holiday, and Cathy said _____ had been great.

4. a) You invited a friend to go out with you to the theatre this evening to see 'Hamlet'. Your friend didn't want to go and made three or four excuses. What did he/she say?

b) You had an interview yesterday for a job in the police force. What did the interviewers ask you?